Henry Clay Mabie

In Brightest Asia

Henry Clay Mabie

In Brightest Asia

ISBN/EAN: 9783744755597

Printed in Europe, USA, Canada, Australia, Japan

Cover: Foto ©Andreas Hilbeck / pixelio.de

More available books at **www.hansebooks.com**

In Brightest Asia

by Henry C. Mabie. D.D.

FIFTH EDITION.
17654

BOSTON:
W. G. CORTHELL, PUBLISHER.
1893.

To the Central Baptist Church,

MINNEAPOLIS,

Which called me to its pastorate in the avowed hope that it might be further incited

To World-Wide Relationships,

which loyally supported me in

Manifold Aggressive Missionary Undertakings,

and which at length unselfishly released me to make this tour of mission-fields and to enter upon an undivided service in the cause of

Evangelizing the Whole Earth,

these sketches, many of which were written for its comfort, are affectionately inscribed.

PREFACE.

IN May, 1890, the writer of these sketches was chosen Home Secretary of the American Baptist Missionary Union. Immediately thereafter, it was provided that, before entering upon official service at home, he should be permitted to make a tour of the mission-fields, especially in Asia. This was to be in no sense a deputation for official examination or the exercise of authority in the missions; but simply an errand of friendly visitation, for the purpose of first-hand observation, inquiry and study respecting the nature, difficulties and promise of the work, the claims of which the writer was expected widely to advocate. This tour was begun in August, 1890, and completed in April, 1891. The countries traversed in order were, Japan, China, Malaysia, Burma, Assam and India, briefly touching Egypt, Palestine, Italy, France and England. About 200 of our own missionaries were visited. The stay in each country was necessarily short. Only certain representative stations in any of the countries could be reached. Some of the more important, including our old mission in Siam, were regretfully passed by altogether. These sketches were written mainly in the form of letters to the various home denominational papers, to family friends, and to the church of my late charge.

These sketches were not intended to express judicial estimates on the relative importance of the various missions nor the quality of work done therein. They did not attempt to discuss theories of missions or mission policies. Their aim was rather to depict, in as graphic a way as possible, some of the characteristic phenomena attending mission life and work in the various countries, with the hope that readers at home would thus be quickened to think of missions more as a reality. The fact that many of our most devoted and skilful workers are not so much as named in these pages, while others are prominently spoken of, is by no means to be construed as indifference to the work of any; much less as unfriendly discrimination against, or disparagement of such work. The writer simply depicts fragments of the work as he saw them. As to other portions, he is silent simply because he did not see them, or had not time, in the haste of travel, to write of them. Others in the past have spoken, and in the future will speak, of these works and the workers as they so well deserve.

What has been written was thrown off amid the hurry of travel, and in the heat of interest awakened on the spots. For the most part, the sketches here appear substantially as they were originally written. They claim to be only glimpses of parts of the work. Nevertheless, they are glimpses of fairly and widely representative parts.

The writer has chosen to entitle these sketches "In Brightest Asia," not because there is not much in Asia yet to be seen of exceeding darkness, but because the traveller among the missions of the Orient, if indeed he has eyes to see, will find that the track along which gospel missionaries have passed and wrought, is an illuminated track. The lights on the otherwise dark scenes of heathenism are all the brighter from the contrast. Moreover, this side of Asiatic life is conscientiously emphasized for the reason that, in the belief of the writer, there is usually but little profit to be drawn from dwelling long upon the dark side of anything. The chief incitements to evangelical work are derived from the positive hope of begetting the "new man," rather than from suppressing the "old,"—from brooding *over* men, in expectation of the second Adam to be formed in them, rather than from brooding *about* the ruined product of the first Adam. So it is believed that with all we are hearing in our day, in mission literature and appeal, about "Darkest Africa," "Darkest England" and "Darkest India,"—and they are not painted darker than they are,—it is time that the lights, also, on the deeply shadowed pictures should be newly pointed out.

"Whatsoever things are true, whatsoever things are honest, whatsoever things are just, whatsoever things are pure, whatsoever things are lovely, whatsoever things are of good report; if there be any virtue, and if there be any praise, think on these things." In Japan, China and India the times are at hand of which the prophet wrote: "The people which sat in darkness saw great light, and to them which sat in the region and shadow of death, light is sprung up."

BOSTON, JAN. 10, 1892.

Henry C. Mabie.

CONTENTS

CHAPTER		PAGE
I.	To the Field. — Severing Ties. — Denver. — Over Marshall Pass. — The Great American Desert. — The Sierras. — A San Francisco Welcome	9
II.	From Occident to Orient. — Through the "Golden Gate." — Mid Pacific. — Nearing Japan	14
III.	In the Sunrise Kingdom. — Yokohama. — Tokio. — Treaty Revision. — Nikko. — Sendai. — Off for Kobe. — Kioto. — Lights and Shadows. — Shimonoseki and Chofu. — Nagasaki	19
IV.	A Buddhist Doctrine of Justification by Faith	40
V.	In the Chinese Empire. — Arrival at Shanghai. — Shanghai as a Base of Operations	43
VI.	The Eastern China Mission. — A Foot-Boat Trip. — A Ningpo Household. — Shaohing. — A Noted Tomb	52
VII.	Up the Yang-tse-Kiang. — Visit to Nanking. — Among Raw Celestials. — A Gifted Missionary. — River Scenery. — Hankow and Griffith John	59
VIII.	Can the Chinese be Christianized? — An Aged Believer. — A Young Mandarin. — A Blind Christian Boy	67
IX.	The Western China Mission. — The Country and Modes of Travel. — Sz-Chuen and the Mission. — Messrs. Upcraft and Warner	70
X.	The Southern China Mission. — Hongkong. — Arrival at Swatow. — Inland on the Swatow Field. — Chao-chow-fu. — A Quaint Bridge. — The Hakkas,	75

CHAPTER	PAGE
XI.—CANTON AND MACAO.—Life in Boats.—Mission of the Southern Baptist Convention.—Macao.—The Tomb of Morrison	87
XII.—MEDICAL MISSION WORK IN CHINA.—The Claim Made for it.—How it Works.—The Present Status.—Results	91
XIII.—EQUATORIAL ASIA.—French China.—Singapore.—American Methodist Mission.—Mohammedanism.—Penang.—Under the Southern Cross.—Rangoon Sighted	96
XIV.—ON BURMAN SOIL.—Visit to Maulmein.—Amherst and Mrs. Judson's Grave.—The Bassein Mission.—The Burman State Railway.—Mandalay.—Ava the Golden.—Judson Memorial Chapel.—Oung-pen-la.—A Karen Association.—Our Shan Mission.—Pegu	107
XV.—THREE VETERANS.—Rev. D. L. Brayton.—Mrs. Cephas Bennett.—Mrs. E. A. Stevens	134
XVI.—INDIA.—Calcutta.—Europeanized India.—Serampore	138
XVII.—OUR ASSAM MISSION.—The Garos.—The Plains People.—The Nagas.—A Meeting with the Brahmo Somaj.—From Calcutta to Bombay.—Bombay,	142
XVIII.—ON THE TELUGU FIELD.—The Deccan.—Work for Eurasians.—Conference at Nellore.—Ramapatam.—Ongole.—Interview with Brahmins.—Off to Camp at Chendalur.—Baptizing Experiences.—The Cumbum Pentecost.—An Impending Crisis	152
XIX.—IN BIBLE LANDS.—Arabian Sea.—Red Sea and Mount Sinai.—Alexandria.—Cairo.—Off for Jaffa.—The Ride to Jerusalem.—In the Holy City.—View from Olivet.—Bethany.—Bethlehem.—Ramleh.—The True Crusade	167

CHAPTER I.

To the Field!

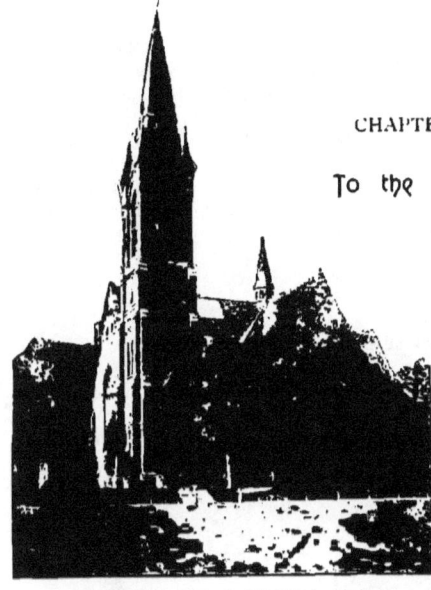

CENTRAL CHURCH, MINNEAPOLIS.

HABITUATED for twenty-one years to the pastoral relation, it was no easy thing to sever the bond. However, many lines of providential circumstance, wide concurrence of the judgments of the brethren, many promptings of the Spirit within, and strong fellowships with the missionaries on the field united to indicate duty: so that at the last there could be no good ground for hesitation to surrender the charge of even such a church as the Central of Minneapolis for the new relation into which the writer had been called.

As for the church, for years it had been growing into Christ-like magnanimity. Why, then, should it not lend its pastor to the Lord, and to the cause it loved? Both work and worker are still theirs in a larger sense. The church has simply more heavily invested in the supreme undertaking — the evangelization of the whole earth.

In pursuance, then, of the suggestion and provision made by certain large-minded friends, the writer of these sketches was despatched to the fields.

Severing Ties.

On a midsummer evening in August, 1890, in the new Social Rooms of the church above mentioned in Minneapolis, was held a farewell meeting with the departing pastor and a member of the church who was to accompany him as far as Japan. A large assemblage of friends was gathered. Graceful tributes in verse, song and address indicated the tender affection and mutual interest which had characterized past relations. On the morning following, the farewells in the family circle were said, and the world-round tour was begun.

Wednesday, August 13, found us *en route* for the Pacific coast, booked to sail by the "City of Peking," August 23, for Yokohama, Japan. The purpose is, if the Lord will, to visit in turn our stations in Japan, China, Burma, Assam and India; thence homeward via Bombay, Suez, Jerusalem, Beirut, Italy, France and England, in time for the next May anniversaries.

Two gifted and earnest missionaries under appointment to Japan, viz., Miss Mead of Minnesota and Miss Blunt of Kansas City, journey with us. They have been missionaries of the first water in the home-land. They are proving themselves such all along the way, — on train, in hotel and steamer, — ever reaching out in tender offices in behalf of their Lord; harbinger this of good and effective work in Sendai and Shimonoseki, Japan. Rev. H. B. Waterman volunteers his companionship, at individual expense. Besides these, Brother Ernest Gordon, son of Dr. A. J. Gordon of Boston, is to join us at San Francisco.

Denver.

On our arrival at Denver, we found that by kind arrangement of Dr. Tupper and others, the whole Sabbath at the First Church had been set apart to us. The ladies held a large meeting in the afternoon, at which our two missionaries tenderly rehearsed their mission call and conviction. Dr. H. A. Tupper, secretary of the Foreign Board of the Southern Convention, providentially present, pathetically and eloquently responded on behalf of the meeting. The writer preached in the morning, and in the evening addressed a large mass meeting on "Missions," speaking of their spirit, their fellowships, their fascinations and their extension. A generous share was taken by the Denver brethren in the expense account of the secretary's tour.

Over Marshall Pass.

August 19.

This has been a day of experiences altogether *sui generis*. Starting from Salida at 7 A.M., the first stretch of the journey was the ascent of the mountains — the real Rockies.

Our train is divided into two sections, each section drawn by two engines, and we start on the ascent over Marshall Pass. In going about twenty miles, we rise 3,000 feet. At first we are under the clouds; then we are in the midst of them;

GARDEN OF THE GODS.

at length we rise above them, and see them rolling away along the sides of the ranges opposite us. Our way is tortuous and serpentine, round and round the lesser heights, up grades so steep that it reminds us of a toboggan slide. We dash through repeated snow sheds, and then emerging from the smoke and cinders, we rise into the purest and thinnest atmosphere. We grow giddy at the sensations of the vast altitude; and from our perch on lofty ledges, the eye scans the vast stretches of the Rocky ranges, rolling, tumbling and Alp-like, soaring still above and beyond into the illimitable ether. We are favored all day with a glorious sunshine which floods everything with its own radiance, and softens and makes tender what otherwise would be an endless and tumultuous array of awfulness.

MT. OURAY.

Marshall Pass is fairly Alpine, though to our surprise there is on none of the peaks at this time of the year much snow, though they rise to upwards of 14,000 feet in height.

At noon we reach the summit; and midway between two lofty horns or peaks, — Mt. Ouray and Mt. Sniffel, — our train comes to a halt; and we all rush out to take in the view Pacificward, which stretches away for 100 miles or so westward.

The Great American Desert.

Leaving Gunnison, quite a flourishing town, ranges of hillocks on every side begin to show sandy, gravelly and indescribably barren. One would think it never rained here. It is a fit region to be traversed with camels. The sun is lurid over it all; the soil, red and ochre yellow; the formations of rocks and mountains, weird, bald and awful. Not even will the sage brush or cactus grow in much of this region.

We are threading a great plain of desert through windings like a ram's horn. We pass for miles and miles between pillared cliffs and overhanging banks of reddish, and at times, yellow sandstone, and greenish, crumbly shales, and both betimes shot through with a garnet-colored trap-rock or porphyritic limestone. Oh, so desolate and chaotic!

Now a sand storm comes down upon us like a simoom, enveloping our train completely. It sifts into our car, filling eyes, mouth and nostrils. The Sahara could not be a wilder waste. It would seem the devil's country. Good old Father Raymond used to say: "The devil was a squatter from the beginning; he never owned an acre in God's earth." I think he might have claimed this region, with none to dispute the claim.

One thing has grown upon me all day; viz., this: That the terms in which we often hear our big country described — and especially the statement that the populations which our great West is capable of sustaining will soon be myriads — are largely wild extravagance. Some say, for instance, that by the year 2000 we shall have 600,000,000 of people in the United States. The Great American Desert is still a stupendous fact, and will always be a vast chasm in the midst of the North American continent.

The Sierras.

August 21.

To-day we are mounting the Sierra Nevada passes, following the course of the Truckee River. How refreshing the green of such a valley after the long, dreary stretch of desert waste! Lumbering camps begin to appear; and now, in the glowing afternoon, as we pass over to the California side, we are amid the sometime famous gold diggings. Disused water flumes and ditches are seen in great frequency. Vast yellow surfaces on all the mountain-sides lie exposed where the hydraulic processes have washed down even the everlasting hills.

Our missionary sisters have meanwhile struck a mine of rarer wealth. A theatre troupe yesterday attached two coaches to our train. These sisters have found their way among the actresses, and are laboring to dissuade them from the allurements of such a career, pointing them Christward. In that deep, dark mine, like merchantmen, they seek for goodly pearls. God bless and reward their search.

SAN FRANCISCO HARBOR.

San Francisco.

August 23.

We reached the city of the Golden Gate on Thursday night. Good Dr. Hartwell, for seventeen years a missionary in China, and now engaged in the best of missionary work in Chinatown, and Mr. Dorsey met us on arrival, and quartered us at the Occidental Hotel.

To the Field.

Next day delegations representing the ministers' meeting and the Women's Society of this coast, called upon us, proffering service of every kind, anticipatory of our sailing on the morrow. We were given a glimpse of heathenism at home, in a walk through Chinatown.

In the afternoon and evening special services of welcome and farewell were held in the First Church, Rev. J. Q. A. Henry, pastor. Dr. Hartwell presided. Misses Blunt and Mead, in their own melting and spiritual way, addressed us as only outgoing missionaries can. The writer followed in a half-hour address on the conditions under which so high work can be happily and well undertaken. The meeting of old friends, such as Brothers Abbott, Rieman and others, added pathos to all. To-morrow at 1.30 o'clock we are to sail.

CHAPTER II.

From Occident to Orient.

Through the "Golden Gate."

On Board the "City of Peking," August 23.

"**H**AUL in the gang plank!" The moment has arrived when we are to say good-by to native land. Captain Cavarly is on deck — square-built, benevolent, though firm. We have some fifty saloon passengers, and numberless Chinese in the steerage. Some of them, alas! being sent back to China for violation of the " Exclusion Act." We have about a dozen missionaries of various boards. A throng of San Francisco friends gather on the wharf. They have filled our staterooms with flowers and fruits. They wish us *bon voyage*, and sing farewell songs. Many an eye is moistened as our vessel swings out into the stream.

The song, "God be with you till we meet again," floats out over the widening breach. Whether that meeting will be on earth or only in heaven, God knows. So long as we can recognize an outline of the dear forms who wave their handkerchiefs, we, too, stand and wave responsively. We round the point, pass through the " Golden Gate," send back by the pilot the hastily penned missives to dear ones far away, and our prow is set towards the Orient world.

GOLDEN GATE.

Mid-Pacific, August 30.

Verily, this is " the wide, wide sea," so desolate, so little traversed, that since the second day out, when we met several coasting vessels and parted company with the Australian steamer which left the " Golden Gate " with us, we have not seen a sail nor even a porpoise. We shipped on the " City of Peking," and frequently have we felicitated ourselves on our providential choice. The vessel has been sixteen years in the service, and has made sixty-five trips between San Francisco and Hong Kong.

Captain John M. Cavarly is the able and vigilant commander. We have a good table and polite stewards, all Japanese and Chinese. One could ask for nothing better.

The crew are all Chinamen. No Cunarder could muster more expert seamen; everything on deck and below is managed with such skill and quietness, that one would suppose the vessel ran itself. We have not heard a harsh command nor an oath indulged in, except by one or two vulgar passengers, since we came on board.

This is our second Sunday at sea. We are now nearly half-way across the Pacific. The weather has been fine — only one day of rain; no fog, and as a rule daily sunshine. Instead of the cold of the Atlantic, we have had no use for heavy wraps. This morning we

ON THE "PEKING."

had a religious service in the social hall. I preached on "That they lay hold on the life which is life indeed." (1 Tim. vi. 19.) [Rev. Ver.]

Captain Cavarly attended, and thanked me warmly for the sermon. We have found most people on board inclined to sneer at all missionaries and their undertakings. Some patience is called for, and it is important to exercise it under such circumstances. I think some were led this morning to see that there are higher ideas of life than those which some of our fellow-travellers represent — pleasure seekers, traders with oriental houses, and shippers of Chinese coolies. We hope for less sneering during the rest of the voyage. We had several Chinese and Japanese at service, and they were among our most attentive listeners. Two of these especially give evidence of being genuine Christians — Lo Jo, the Chinese boy, and Mr. Abe, the Japanese boy. The latter I found yesterday in the prow of the ship, flat down on his stomach, reading the Acts of the Apostles. His shipmates were gaming near by him. Both these boys have often joined us at evening worship. The former told us his experience one evening.

I am just finishing reading Carpenter's "Self-support in Bassein," a book full of information and wisdom on mission work, despite its severe criticisms. He gives high praise to Mr. Beecher, and especially brings out the great worth and genius of E. L. Abbott, a man of whom I had previously known little, I am ashamed to say. The book has deepened my interest to see Burma. It has also led me to realize how very difficult is the task of a true foreign missionary. What nerve and grace and staying powers it requires!

I am impressed that much of our modern enthusiasm among the young people at home is superficial, and will require thorough chastening. Perhaps the sad taking-off of those " Independents " to the Soudan has reference to this. Whole-hearted as was their devotion, this work is unquestionably the highest and therefore fraught with the greatest difficulties of any work on earth. Yesterday we crossed the 180th parallel of longitude; so we are now in the Orient, and dropped out Tuesday from our calendar. We are ahead of you at last.

Nearing Japan.

Wednesday Morning, September 10, 6 A.M.

We are just sailing up the bay, a few miles out from Yokohama. We are up early to see the sun rise on his own kingdom. There he comes, golden and regal, over yonder jagged and wonderfully picturesque line of mountains. The whole coast on either side is a mass of islands

ENOSHIMA.

and promontories, peaked as the edge of a saw, serpentine, and everywhere appearing volcanic. A few trees stand like crests on the summits. Clouds of fog bank are rolling up from the interior bays and mountain valleys. Fishing-smacks lie in groups at intervals along the bay. It seems refreshing, indeed, to see land again after seventeen days. These shores mark the outline of the province of Kadzusa. What tales they could tell if they could but speak of aboriginal life! A shout goes up from our port side, and our missionary girls are running and exclaiming, "Oh, there is Fujiyama! I have caught the first view of Fujiyama!"—the sometimes snow-crowned, conical-shaped sacred mount, the Hermon of the empire, 12,000 feet high. It is sixty miles away, and not always seen by any means by incoming steamers. But from beginning to end we have been favored. The square-sailed, junk-like boats of the country now appear with high-turned prow and stern. Our girls adopt the land at sight, and are elated and joyful, with song and dancing eyes. They have just come up from below, where they say they have been giving themselves up in fresh devotion to the redemption of this "Land

FUJIYAMA.

of the Morning," this Aurora of the Orient. Oh, that here the gospel indeed may ride Aurora-like before the dawn of divine illumination for sublime but idolatry-stricken old Asia.

A coast town, with little, low, tiled roofs, now comes into view, just nestled under the loveliest hills, on one of which a large, square-built white lighthouse appears. But as Miss B. is suggesting, there is one sad lack: "No church spire rises from amid the village." Now we are passing a fishing-boat in which are three men who forgot to put on their clothes when they got up this morning. They look as if they could live in the water about as well as on land. We are now passing the little village of Uraga, at which Commodore Perry first landed when he was making his treaty with Japan. Now we are making fast to our steamer buoy,—there being no wharves,—and numberless boats of the half-naked natives, and several steam launches are approaching to take us off. Among the latter is one from the United States flag-ship "Omaha," which lies here; and Lieutenant Murdock steps on board, whom I recognize from his resemblance to his father. Five minutes later, and three of our bright missionaries, Brothers Dearing, Harrington and Hamblen, approach with a steam launch to take us off. A few minutes suffice to get our baggage through the customs. Then we each take a jinrikisha, and off our men trot in a procession of us through the town and up the hill to the noble and picturesque "Bluff," embowered in trees to Miss Britton's missionary boarding-house, where we soon find ourselves disposed in the most comfortable and homelike quarters. How strangely quaint and picturesque everything is, as if we had landed on a new planet!

A scene of bewildering natural loveliness spreads itself about on every side. We are perched on a romantic hillside terraced into the most charming gardens, sloping down to a serpentine strip of lowland on which fields of green growing rice are standing, with ditches running through and through them. Beyond that are other slopes rising gradually and in broken undulations, traversed by ravines for miles away On these slopes are small farms and gardens, cultivated to the highest pitch conceivable. To the right and the left are the other European residences, each on its beautiful terrace, bewitching with vistas and copses and shaded nooks. Then such varieties of foliage, shrub and plant one who has not been here or in the tropics cannot imagine. It is all like enchanted ground.

A number of missionaries are here, including Dr. and Mrs. Ashmore, so we are by no means lonesome. All are in good health and spirits. There is some cholera, especially in the western parts, but wholly among the lower-class natives. It has not touched Europeans, and what there is, is under good control.

JAPANESE GARDEN.

CHAPTER III.

In The Sunrise Kingdom.

Yokohama.

THIS is our oldest station. Here it was that Dr. Brown, Mr. Poate and others first began Baptist work. On the famous "Bluff," a bold spur of rock stretching for a mile or two along the southwest side of the city, and completely embowered in the foliage of a hundred varieties of trees, in the foreign concession, reside our missionaries amidst some hundreds of other foreigners. Mrs. Ashmore, formerly Brown, has a home here; so also have Mr. Bennett and Mr. C. K. Harrington; and here we found Mr. J. L. Dearing, our latest accession to the force in Yokohama. Four sisters are also here engaged in school work — Misses Converse, Rolman, Wilson and Church. Our Theological Seminary is here, under the charge of Rev. A. A. Bennett, one of our oldest missionaries. He was in some sense the successor to Dr. Nathan Brown, especially in educational lines. He is just now absent in America, and much missed, especially by the writer, of whom he was a classmate in the seminary, and who would have been glad to meet Brother Bennett at home. Here, also, lives Kaukatzu san, our senior

GIRLS' SCHOOL, YOKOHAMA.

ordained native pastor, who assisted Dr. Brown through eleven years in translating the Scriptures. He has rendered help in the seminary, and is to-day our most valuable native preacher and interpreter. He was my companion for an entire week in my trip to the North, and won my heart completely.

The second day after arrival, I was invited over to the Ashmores', where I have been staying until to-day. Dr. Ashmore has poured out a flood of information and wisdom combined on all the mission problems, and we have had long and profitable talks. There is a vast amount of rainy, steamy weather, which keeps one in a constant vapor bath; but a change for cooler is expected at any time. They say it never fails to come about the middle of September.

Last Sunday I attended my first service in a native church, and heard a sermon from one of the native pastors. It was very touching to see the little congregation of about sixty persons engaging in the various parts of the service. Every head bowed during prayer, all saying the "Amen" at the close. All sang with much earnestness, giving absolute attention to the end; no looking about; and as the minister concluded, the whole congregation bowed as if to say, "Thank you." At 4 o'clock came the Sunday school, and in the evening I went with Mr. Dearing to attend an evangelistic service just started at the house of his teacher.

A Japanese house is peculiar. The whole front opens, by means of sliding doors, to the street. As you go in, there is a space of say three feet wide stretching across the front on the ground. Here you are expected to remove your shoes before climbing up on the floor, two and one-half feet higher. This floor is not of boards, but is entirely overlaid with mats of rice straw, softly padded underneath, and each mat about three by six feet in size, which at night constitutes the mattress on which the family sleep. They are so clean that they must not be soiled, and so delicately made that the nails and heels of our boots would cut them out; so we either sit in our stocking feet, or put on little straw sandals which they furnish us. The people all bend their lower limbs and feet back under them, and sit on them. They never have chairs, except in occasional instances for guests.

When you are seated, first, the woman of the house and then all the children crawl up to you and bow down to the very floor before you in a salutation. Of course on this occasion, I rose and bowed my lowest, and smiled my blandest. When the service began with singing, the house being open, a crowd gathered at once before the door, some of the people sitting on the side of the elevated floor within. Thus for half an hour a large number stood and listened to the gospel. The text was written on a long white scroll, in Chinese and Japanese characters, and hung on the wall beside and behind the preacher, which of itself was an impressive thing.

Tokio.

SAN JU NI BAHN, TSUKIJI, September 20.

Here at the great capital numbering over 1,000,000 souls, we have three male missionaries and their wives: viz. Brethren F. G. Harrington, G. W. Taft and J. C. Brand. Brother Fisher is about returning from America. These are all diligently working at the language, and, through native assistants, coming into such evangelistic relation to the people at the several preaching-stations as they are able. Here also Miss Kidder and Miss Clagett are at work in the girls' school, one of the very brightest spots to be seen in our Japan work. Christian training is telling here; and indirectly, men, as well as women, are being constantly reached and renewed by the gospel's power, as brought to them through the tact and indefatigable zeal of these consecrated women. They reminded us of Paul's frequent allusions to "those other women, helpers in the Lord." In the near neighborhood of this school, we saw the chief activities among the native churches. Here we partook with some of them of the Lord's Supper. Here we saw three generations of believers, including several preachers and Bible-women, in a single family. But Tokio is just now seething with political excitement. Here congregate the thousands of student youths of Japan, often but a synonym for conceited rowdies who, under the name of *Soshii*, seek to browbeat the government and intimidate the populace. The prejudice against foreigners runs very high. There is frequent violence used against them. Mission movements just now have to proceed on very cautious lines, and it is not to be wondered at that many of our workers feel depressed. We have had the cheering experience, together with Brother and Sister Brand, of examining four candidates, whom we received and baptized on the following Sunday evening. Their convictions proved surprisingly clear and their testimony emphatic.

Our Baptist workers are among the youngest really to begin operations on this field. They are diligently acquiring the language, familiarizing themselves with the habits of the people, providing mission-houses in which they can safely and suitably dwell, and opening preaching and teaching stations, where converts may be gathered and trained. We have attended several of the native services on the Sabbath and week nights, and been touched by the close attention and reverence of the hearers, by the heartiness of the singing, and by the earnestness with which the native preachers have pressed home the claims of Christ. The frequent gatherings with the missionaries for special prayer and Scripture incitement to a more aggressive evangelism in which the Spirit's power may be expected and evinced have proved refreshing and inspiring to us all. It strikes us that generally in Japan, there has been far too much of reliance upon the outward visible tendencies of the Japanese to adopt Western civilization in the husk. The time of testing is at hand, and the church of God in Japan will be brought to its knees; much of misdirection in method will be confessed, the Holy Spirit will be more mightily invoked, and divine influence will show its old-time reality and power.

If any have adopted Japan as a sort of easy-going mission-field, they will be disabused of the delusion, clarified by the discipline imminent, and rise to truer mission work. The talk about "The immediate Christianization of Japan" has about ceased. The carnal heart may be illusively polite among these Frenchmen of the East; but for its subduing and renewal, it will require the same almighty grace that has always been required to operate effectually upon the citadel of Mansoul anywhere. Mighty prayer only can bring it.

I have done a deal of sight-seeing in and about Tokio, staying at the Brands', most earnest, spiritual and aggressive evangelistic people. Mrs. Brand was formerly Miss Sands, and, having been long in the country and skilled in the language, is wonderfully well informed. Mr. Brand, while studying hard on the language, has gathered about him several native workers, and is plunging right into evangelizing through interpreters.

This is so different a world from anything we have known! Think of 3,000 Buddhist and Shinto temples in Tokio alone! The craze for education, secular and European, as yet is almost wholly inimical, in the judgment of some, to mission work. The Japanese who are partly educated have grown correspondingly conceited and arrogant, and are fairly crowding their former teachers out of their positions.

To look at the great public buildings, banks, railway stations, government institutions, etc.,

MR. BRAND AND ASSISTANTS.

you might think yourself in Europe; but then again, when you go through the streets swarming with half-naked, hatless natives, upon whom elements of Western civilization have been thrust uninvited by them, you have a mongrel combination. They are heathen still, and in gross darkness.

BELL TOWER.

Treaty Revision.

The air, politically speaking, is full of treaty revision. It is the irrepressible conflict, and well it may be. The first treaties, made, not as is commonly said by Commodore Perry, but by our first United States minister, Townsend Harris, five years after Perry opened the port at Yokohama, were in important particulars in their inception a blunder; and upon that blunder as a basis, Lord Elgin and representatives of the other powers followed in a species of crafty diplomacy which ever since has proved — and more and more as time has elapsed — that we really closed Japan in the very act of opening it.

Undoubtedly Minister Harris designed to deal fairly with Japan; but by grave oversight, which till his death he never ceased to deplore, there were points in his treaty which unwittingly did Japan serious wrong, and which he sought too late to remedy. Thus our treaty, the first

PLACE OF COMMODORE PERRY'S LANDING.

made with Japan, with all its wrongs to Japan expanded, so as to afford to outside nations commercial advantages of untold value, giving nothing whatever in return, was promptly seized upon by Western powers. By what is known as "the most favored nation clause," these treaties were rendered practically interminable — made so by the item introduced by Lord Elgin and copied by all the powers, that "any concession granted to any government by Japan for any privileges, however valuable, may be claimed at once by all the powers, without any concession in return to Japan whatever."

This has always stood, since 1858, a complete bar against Japan making or revising her own treaties. The chief incidental evil in this grew out of the fact that England secured from

Japan a concession that a duty of only 5 per cent should be collected on imported goods from any nation whatever. Mr. Harris had proposed a duty of 20 per cent. This England's minister foiled, and the twenty-eight powers now in commercial relations with Japan took advantage of it, and still retain it. Japan is in great financial straits in consequence.

The commerce and industries of Japan being throttled, the tariff being held to such a minimum, the taxes for government support are forced back on the land. I am told it actually takes one half the farmer's product to pay the government taxes, and one quarter more is required to pay the land owner, leaving the man who tills the soil only one quarter of his product of silk or rice or cotton on which to live. Is it any wonder, then, that there is at last in Japan, with all its awakening intelligence and moral sense, an uprising in protest?

What is called the anti-foreign feeling and the reaction against Western influence is due, as I divine it, mainly to the waking realization of Japan to the toils into which the shrewd powers of the West have drawn her. A vigorous struggle, late as it is, to defend herself against universal oppression and national undoing, is the result.

The secular educational *furore* has unquestionably been at white heat. For years there has been an importation of all the advanced speculative theorizings from Germany, France, England and America, touching education. Every man aspires to be a philosopher, a Spencer, a Mill, or Hegel — no matter who, if he is only much talked of abroad.

It would be untrue, however, to suppose that the anti-foreign feeling now prevalent, though arising mainly from resistance to the treaty status, is the whole truth. Japan has for twenty years been going too fast. She has been much flattered, both at home and abroad. In many cases the Japanese have come to overvalue themselves and their acquisitions, until now there is a wide feeling that henceforth they can go alone, and little thanks to either foreign money or foreign instruction. There are some painful cases of such ingratitude, toward even their chief benefactors, among all the missions. Doubtless a sifting process is needed, and it probably is at hand.

Nikko. October 5.

Nikko is one of the Meccas of Japan. It has been a sacred place since A. D. 767, when the Buddhist saint, Shodo Shodon, first visited it. Early in the seventeenth century it was selected by the second Shogun as a resting-place for his father, Iyeyasu, the first Shogun. A great procession accompanied the remains of Iyeyasu on a journey of nearly a month from Suruga, in Southern Japan, to Nikko. Iyemitsu, the third Shogun, is also here entombed, and likewise deified.

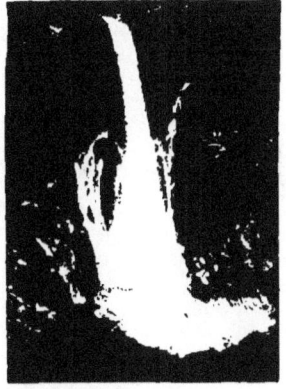

KEGON NOTAKI WATERFALL.

Thus you see this is the seat of a great national shrine — a sort of Westminster Abbey. To it vast numbers of devoted pilgrims are always coming, and especially at the time of the great festivals.

CRYPTOMERIAS.

One of the impressive things about the establishment of this place is the canonization of the very road by which the remains of Iyeyasu were brought to this spot. Our ride for twenty-six miles was along this road. Think of two rows of trees, immense lofty pines or cedars, from two to five feet in diameter, about 150 feet in height, the branches of which completely over-arch the road, and a stream of clear mountain spring water flowing on each side of this road at the roots of the trees. The road itself is smooth and hard, trodden for ages. Through this we rode all the afternoon, and about 6 o'clock we drove up to the most comfortable of native inns, where many missionaries on their summer outings have been stopping.

The surroundings of Nikko are as mountainous and picturesque as those of Lauterbrunnen, in Switzerland. Waterfalls, springs and dashing torrents are on every side; and the terraced hills, with their matchless costly and magnificent temples and shrines, are fairly bewildering. A very interesting "Sacred Bridge" crosses the Daiya Gawa, a rushing stream just below the wondrous temples which stand on the terraces above.

The great excursion of the neighborhood is up to Lake Chuzenji and Yumoto, twelve and sixteen miles right up the

SACRED BRIDGE, NIKKO.

mountain-sides. At Yumoto we were 4,800 feet above the sea, and there were lofty peaks and extinct volcanoes 3,000 feet higher all around us. This trip we took during the last two days and in the most ideal weather. The mountain lakes so high up and filled with salmon trout, — on some of which we feasted, — are so crystalline and green, the lookouts from lofty precipices are so bold, and the little tea-houses perched on crags, with the ruddy little Japanese maids who sit on their feet ready to wait on you while you eat, form scenes so uniquely picturesque, that the surprise and delight of each stage of the journey are without parallel in anything which I have seen. At Yumoto there are hot boiling sulphur springs, in the water of which all tourists bathe before retiring for the night, — a preparation for sleep after the long day's horseback-riding, climbing and boating to get there, not to be despised.

LAKE CHUZENJI.

It would have amused you to see the motherly old woman who waited on my table give me lessons in the use of chopsticks, which I resolutely undertook for once. Fortunately for the soup, I had in my pocket one of the spoons which was put up with my lunch when I left home. That spoon is serving me many a good turn. To the natives in these wilds it is like Joseph's cup — a thing to conjure with. It was a fine expression of Oriental hospitality, the next morning, when the old bald patriarch of the house picked up our baggage and escorted us to the gate of the town, at which, when he had arrived, he faced about, and, giving us our effects, bowed with his face almost touching the ground, and saying, " Saya-nara " (i. e., " Good-by "), sent us on our way.

We have had as one of our companions here Mr. Liddiard of Hastings, England, one of the finest of English Christian laymen, and a great Sunday-school man of the Jacobs type. He was at the late Pittsburgh Sunday-school convention. He has travelled widely, and is out now for two years of it. I much enjoy him. Thus friends turn up on all hands to those who are in the Lord's way.

This morning we had a little service in English in one of the rooms. Only five were present, Mr. L., Mr. W., two Japanese preachers, my man Kaukatza and a fine seminary student from the Congregational school of Kioto, and myself. Mr. W. preached on " Who hath created of one blood all nations," etc. Mr. L. prayed. We all sang. " Come, let us join our cheerful songs " and " Jesus shall reign where'er the sun." Following the sermon, I prayed, being specially led out for the two evangelists with us, and for Japan as a whole. It was a tender time. The spirit of the Lord drew near, and we all felt it good thus to meet and worship Him — England, America and Japan represented. N. was visibly affected, and I am sure I was to an unusual degree. Oh, for a down-pour on these dear native preachers. This is my constant burden in Japan. Kaukatza gave us the benediction in his deep, rich Japanese, as follows: "Nega wakuwa *Chichinanu Kamino* megumi *Kimi Yesuro* itsuku shimi *Kiyoki Mitamano* skitashimi tsuneni warerato tomoni arah Koto mo. Amen." This evening these two brethren have called a meeting for the natives to be held in the largest room in the pension. I encouraged them to go out this afternoon from house to house, and get the people stirred up to come in. I trust they will succeed.

YOMEIMON GATE.

They tell us that if they can say that we foreigners will speak to them also, it will bring more. So we hope in this way at least to develop that quality which at home our churches are all eager for, viz., the drawing quality. Oh, but heathenism is dense here, and almost unbroken. There are temples on all sides of us, and gods of stone by the hundreds. Every hour the deep bass gongs and bells, rung by the priests, remind us that, if we are ever to gain this people, there must be put forth efforts of which we have not yet dreamed. There is not a gospel laborer of any kind settled or regularly laboring in this place of several thousands in this Jerusalem of Japan, and it has been called a sacred place for 1,200 years. And yet the people have everything they really need except the gospel.

At the shrine of Iyemitsu we saw a poor, pale Buddhist priest, for whom my heart yearned. His face is the second of two which were sketched in the *Century* a short time ago. Through Kaukatza I asked him if he had ever seen the New Testament of Jesus Christ. He said, "No." I gave him 20 cents with which to buy a copy, telling him it had brought the greatest blessings to me, rest of heart, redemption from sin, and it had blessed millions in my country. He bowed low, and not only thanked me, but promised to get one at once. Twenty minutes afterwards, he came running after us to thank me again, saying he would get the Testament.

Sendai.

Sendai, on the bay of the same name, on the east coast, situated high and dry on a flat above a rushing river, is a city of some 60,000 souls, an important city from every point of view. Brother E. H. Jones and wife and Brother S. W. Hamblen are here; the latter only recently come, but already getting well into use of the language. There is a native church of about 160 members, worshipping in a new, commodious chapel. Several out-stations are in operation. There is a beautiful mission compound of three acres, situated on a picturesque bluff, and a good mission-house built in Japanese style, which Brother Jones occupies, to be supplemented soon, we trust, by another on the same compound for Brother Hamblen. Here, also, are three missionary single ladies — Miss Fife, Miss Phillips, and Miss Mead. The latter came with us from Minnesota. There is under their charge the beginning of a promising work for girls and

OSHIMA VOLCANO.

women. They however greatly need a compound purchased for them, and suitable simple buildings erected for a girls' school and for the training of Bible-women. The seasons of conference and prayer enjoyed with these workers at Sendai will long be tenderly remembered.

It was a great disappointment that, owing to washouts on the railway, we failed to make such connections as to meet Mr. Poate of Morioka, who had been to Sendai and left before we reached the place. We have no better worker in Japan than he.

Off for Kobe. October 7.

This afternoon we are off for Kobe by this new and splendid vessel, the "Kobe Maru." We had quite a leave-taking of the many warm friends we have made in Yokohama.

A fine sight has just called us from the lunch table. A British fleet of nine men-of-war, sailing in two columns or rows, led by the gaily decorated flag-ship of the admiral, are sailing up the bay as we leave it. The ships are all pure white, and make a fine appearance. They will help the Japs to be a little more temperate, pending the excitement of the coming parliament, perhaps, but of course there are no warlike outbreaks expected.

Now, two hours later, we are passing a high, mountainous island called Bresse, the summit of which, Osima, is a perpetual volcano. A cloud of smoke a half-mile in height lies on the mount, and curls away gracefully heavenward; and the western sun smiting it, turns it to a roseate hue, so that you might fancy it kindled from within. It is even more striking, I am told, than Vesuvius in its volume of smoke. Last week we saw another volcano, Fantaisan, on the way to Sendai. A year or so ago the whole side of the mountain blew out in an explosion, the ashes of which fell twenty-five miles away, and it smokes voluminously yet.

A Touch of Earthquake.

We have been treated (?) to three live earthquakes. The first two were trifling. Indeed, the first one I doubted if it were real,—the windows rattling and the lamps vibrating a little. But last night I was sitting on the floor in my room, re-packing my baggage, when suddenly the floor under me heaved as if it were a sea wave, and everything cracked and settled; and then there was a twisting motion, and—well—I have had enough. Once like that will do, especially when you remember that in the past there have been earthquakes which have destroyed thousands of lives and swallowed villages. I began to believe there was a big turtle under the earth, perhaps near Minneapolis, and he thought he would turn over for a change. The earth's crust is a little too thin here for comfort, and no mistake. It makes one more willing to go to sea.

It is very restful again, after four weeks of visiting and sight-seeing, discussing mission policy from every conceivable point of view with missionaries of so varied ideas, and in so diverse circumstances,—dealing with people whose language they cannot acquire under five years,—to get away to sea and have a little sense of leisure. The greatness of the task of successfully conducting these Asiatic missions is beyond any possible estimate that can be formed at home.

KOBE, October 8.

We landed here this afternoon at 4 o'clock, and find ourselves to-night snugly quartered at the pleasant home of our missionary, R. A. Thomson. This city, with its contiguous city of Hiogo, altogether numbering over 100,000 souls, situated on a bay at the head of the Inland Sea, on its crescent beach, and beneath the picturesque mountains at the back, struck me as one of the most attractive of Japanese cities. Here we found our lone missionary, Brother Thomson, and his sunny wife (the other missionary, Brother Rhees, is at present in America) working away as busily as bees in clover-time. Brother Thomson has the Scotch grit and the Scotch grace, and the training of the Guinnesses of London, which of itself is usually a guarantee of an aggressive and soul-winning evangelism. There was no note of discouragement, no talk of difficulties; but all was for advance. A thriving church; well-attended Sunday services; a capable native pastor and thriving out-stations; and besides, Brother Thomson and his wife have gathered from among the more promising young men employed in the Custom House, the Post Office and the banks, a band of some fifty or sixty whom they teach three evenings weekly, the Bible being most prominent.

On Sunday morning we had gathered a large roomful of them to hear an address on "The Life of Faith." The most of them understood me well without the interpreter. It looked to me as if this brother was rapidly developing a school of evangelists all his own, and of the right sort.

Our week in this less political atmosphere than that found in and about Tokio was an experience full of encouragement. We had here also delightful interviews with Brothers McCullom and Bronson, who have been temporarily here, but who now are to locate in Osaka. These brethren are representatives of the Southern Convention Board. One of the loveliest waterfalls pours down through a glen hard by.

Kioto. October 13.

I have been to Kioto, spending two days, the guest of Dr. Davis, the senior professor in the Doshisha School, founded by Neesima, the American educated Japanese of world-wide fame. Dr. Davis is a graduate of Beloit College and the Chicago Congregational Seminary, and we know many Congregationalists in common. We had a fine visit, and he showed me

WATERFALL AT KOBE.

about the city, the great temples, etc., besides giving me an inside view of the college, the Yale of Japan. Six hundred or more students were at the chapel exercise. They have thirteen dormitories for boys, built in Japanese style, besides the four large brick structures on the main campus, and besides the large girls' school and training-school for nurses. These Congregationalists have taken hold of things, though, in Japan in right good earnest. One of their people, Mr. Harris of New London, Conn., has devoted $100,000 to the Doshisha School. Nothing we have seen of late, save the beaming face of the donor himself, which we had the pleasure of seeing in July at Moody's Northfield College Conference, has done us more good than the sight of the spacious building erected at Kioto by this princely Christian, with what it implies at home and abroad.

NEESIMA.

Where is the Baptist philanthropist who, with similar farsightedness and devotion, will do similar things for us, especially for our theological or training-school? We are happy to note the harbinger of such good things to come from the home beneficence,

KIOTO.

whereby it was made possible for us to participate in the consecration of the new site for the "Mary Colby Girls' Home," just purchased in Yokohama. We were glad to see this decided step forward taken while we were on the ground as the guests of Dr. and Mrs. Ashmore. We trust similar moves, with a far look ahead, may follow in the near future, as the progress in evangelization may warrant them.

Light and Shadows.

KOBE, October 12.

To my dear old church:—

I have returned from Kioto. Here I am in the very thick of the battle, amid the stern and yet glowing realities of the reclamation of great races from heathenism and idolatry, oh, so gross! and not even love for so dear, dear a place as the atmosphere of the Central Church would turn me back. If it were a mere agency of the professional sort, confined to travelling over the country, to asking the people for money, to making sentimental speeches before conventions at home, I could never have left you; but I am now amid the realities and the sublime achievements of the work itself. I face heathenism and its horrible fruits of corruption and death every day. I tread my way through the great avenues, up the massive staircases of stone hollowed by the tread of myriads through the centuries, to temples, numbering from 1,000 to 3,000 in a single city; enthroned on all the bold cliffs, nestled under all the stateliest trees, on all the hillsides that encircle a city (as in Kioto, for thirty miles round), and everywhere I find humanity thronging, prostrating themselves, muttering empty prayers to gilded blocks of images of wood and stone, and turning sorrowfully away as hungry as they came.

But this is not all I see. Were this all, my heart would sink. Another picture presents itself here in divine relief. Little congregations of smiling, radiant worshippers in their plain, simple chapels; native preachers holding in hand the divine transforming word, and pouring their eager testimony into the upturned faces and open hearts before them; Sunday schools singing our own sweet hymns; Christian schools, colleges and theological seminaries, with hundreds of bright-faced and renewed youth, abreast of many in our own home schools in all the elements of Christian learning; sunny kindergartens, with their little marching throngs, hymning their infant devotion in the sweetest strains to our Christ and theirs, all taught, not only by missionaries, but by scores of native teachers, both men and women; young women's seminaries, with girls numbering often 150 or 200 sweet and accomplished characters in a single school.

Ah! there are bright spots in contrast with the vast darkness, that gleam like heavenly stars in the densest night. Daily I am mingling in these scenes, not merely as an onlooker, but as a sharer. I often find opportunity to speak through an interpreter a few words, twice I preached an entire sermon, once I examined four candidates for baptism, and the next night with my own hands baptized them in Christ's name.

To-day I had an opportunity to open conversation so easily with a bright young teacher of some Buddhist students, who also is teaching Japanese to one of our Southern Convention missionaries, and who speaks English well. He said he was "studying Christianity." I cautioned him against studying it as a mere philosophy, and commended to him Christ himself, to be welcomed into the heart, to become a power of peace and blessing inwardly, to be received immediately.

without delay. In short, I pressed him as I would any Minneapolis sinner or agnostic. He winced, grew tender, and acknowledged the obligation. I said: "We may never meet again; let me pray for you here and now." He consented. I poured out my heart for him. At the close he said with emphasis, "Amen." I shook his hand warmly, commended him to the New Testament, and to the God of it, and left him. Mrs. Bronson, who sat by and witnessed it all, thanked me for my interest in their teacher. She said she had been longing to reach him; and for the object lesson on pressing the claims of Christ, she gave me thanks, and now that the ice was broken, promised to follow it up.* I have frequent opportunities of this kind — on the train, steamers, and with jinrikisha men who pull me about the streets; in short, I am far more a missionary than a secretary these days.

JINRIKISHA.

* Before leaving Kobe, I had a second interview with this young man, and had good hope that he had accepted Christ. Afterwards, while in Singapore, I wrote him. Eight months afterwards, when I had reached home, I received the following word from him: "Gentleman,— Your kind favor of December 4 I duly received. Being told that you are now in America, I send an answer to your letter. When I saw you at Mr. T's I realized how Christianity influences the people, and I came to the decisive conclusion that I should profess Christ publicly, before my parents, relatives and friends. But they are not Christians, so on my becoming Christian they would naturally censure me. But, thank God, I was baptized by Mr. McC. at Osaka, and I am now preparing to meet with sneers and scorn. I rely upon God as a strong cane when I feel unable to walk in the path full of brambles and obstacles; as a strength when I feel weak; as a sharp sword when I encounter an enemy. Not only I prepare for their attacking, but for their conversion. One of my brothers-in-law is a very powerful man, who lately became a member of Diet, and who possesses three big news offices; and yet he is not a Christian. If he is converted, indeed 1,000 people shall follow his example. I am going to open a battle of pen with him. Oh, it is fearful when I think about those times when I did not believe Christ, and it is woe to me, as Paul said, if I do not preach to others. But first I will study the Bible. I have many things to tell you, but my poor English would not express my thoughts. God bless you, genuine believer. Yours truly, K. K."

Then you should see how hungry these dear, often lone, and half-discouraged missionaries are for the cheering Bible talks which I am permitted to give; how they run and bring in other missionaries of any and every denomination to share with them in the refreshment. Yesterday we had a sister from Minnesota (Congregationalist), supported by the students of Carleton College; and to-day a Chicago lady, teaching kindergarten; and again this afternoon a woman supported by Plymouth Church, Minneapolis; and this evening a Miss Carr (Methodist), whom I once met at Asbury Park. You should have heard the regret expressed by these Congregational ladies, as they said, "No secretary of the American Board has ever come out to see us, and we so thank you for coming; and you have so helped us by your talk to-day."

And so it goes. I miss, indeed, my precious ones in the home nest and in the home church, but I dare not take long yet to think on that; with my face set to-morrow to go with Brother Halsey to Shimonoseki and Nagasaki, and thence to Shanghai, I look on to other fields with increasing zest, and the certain assurance that I am both sent, and by Christ's grace needed.

We are wofully behind everybody here — so inexcusably behind. The opportunities have been so great; the promise so large; the first beginnings so neglected or allowed to be overgrown with weeds, timid hearts so unencouraged, so few resources drawn upon from the home-land. Things here have so needed unification, melting together through spiritual means, and toning up through the impartation of a larger confidence, both in God and in the denomination's purpose to really wage a campaign in Japan. It is late for Baptists in Japan, but by God's grace we will have a victory yet in this wonderful empire. Such another opportunity does not exist on the planet for rapid and brilliant triumphs of the cross, — not even in North America. Among other things, I want, in Christ's name, $100,000 for Japan in the next three years! You may as well begin to pray for it. You will hear much of special discouragements in Japan just now, but God knows no discouragements. The encouragements far outweigh them in any case.

I have had no time nor heart to-night to speak of the wondrous beauties of the country from end to end; of the fascinations and bewitching features of the whole type of landscape, custom, arts and civilization. For this time you must be content with my

SANJUSENDO TEMPLE.

heart-spillings on deeper things. Besides, I know this is what you want. I am well, happy as a king, and a prophet, too. Give my love to the whole dear family, not only under B's roof, under the parsonage shingles, but also under the whole canopy of the dear old church. Most tenderly and truly,

YOUR PASTOR TILL YOU GET ANOTHER.

I am mailing to you a map of the city of Kioto. The city has 500,000 people. Bear in mind that all those great red square blotches all around on three sides of the city, with spacious park-like grounds, are without exception idolatrous temples; and they are only a part of the thousand or more which the city contains. What do the Baptist unions in American churches think of this as a specimen of church extension? One of these temples has a mammoth image of the Goddess Kwannon, with 1,000 hands and eleven faces; and on each side of her there are 500 other gilded images standing ten rows on a side, each five feet high, — 1,000 in all, and each image has ten small images on each head and ten on each hand. The building containing them is 400 feet long. It is called "The Thirty Thousand God Temple." In one place a new one is building, costing $5,000,000; and yet most of these people are poor beyond description, living on $50 per year. In one of these temples I saw a poor pilgrim making 1,000 rounds of the temple corridor, and casting into a box with each round a little stick, to keep his tally, in order to accumulate merit.

Yes, pray for Japan; and give the gospel to Asia at any cost, *and give it soon*.

Shimonoseki and Chofu.

At the extreme west of the Inland Sea, on the strait opening into the China or Yellow Sea, on the north shore, lies Shimonoseki; and four miles up the coast, lies Chofu. For once, we Baptists have occupied a place first; and in this region we are the only workers. Brother R. L. Halsey is at Shimonoseki, and Brother Shoemaker is about settling in Chofu. In the latter place, three single sisters are occupying the beautiful mission compound, situated on a lovely coast just facing the fairy-like islets in that charming sea, which is studded with myriads of them of every form. Here a girls' school is to be started, under the management of Miss Blunt, who came out in our company. Concerning this school, we have had many seasons of prayer. Miss H. M. Browne has also her work here, chiefly house to house work, as a real missionary; and Mrs. Sharland, an English sister who has had long experience in Burma, as well as in Japan, and who now joins our mission, serving at her own charges, is to lend a hand here in a service much appreciated. Some sixty believers are already enrolled in this district. There are several good evangelists at work here, and some promising licentiates, and numbers of towns on all sides awaiting the coming of the good tidings.

Brother Halsey and I came on together, having a splendid sail of a night and a day in the most perfect weather, through the famous Inland Sea. This sea is a sort of a thousand-island piece of scenery of great magnificence, and many-fold surpassing the beauty and even grandeur of the famous St. Lawrence group. The number of the islands is myriad, and the channels numberless, through which swift-rushing tides run with such violence that the steamer has hard work to make its way. The shapes and configurations of the islands and headlands are numerous. Often you see glistening beaches, golden in the sunshine, and then rocks that frown with blackness, and then lovely terraces on which the wheat and other harvests grow plentifully. Numerous villages sit ensconced on the shores, and look out from the gentlest slopes.

SHIMONOSEKI.

Little harbors are white with many sail of the fishermen, and the white surf bejewels every shore. These islands all rise to a considerable height, their sides are steep, and the summits above them are peaked with jaggedness in miniature outline, altogether characteristic of Japanese mountains. This is undoubtedly the peculiar result of volcanic action in some primeval age, when this whole mass of 3,000 or more islands was thrust up by Omnipotence out of fiery depths. The whole extent of Japan, from the first point at which I caught a view to this southwest coast which we are skirting to-day, presents a succession of those jagged, saw-tooth-shaped mountain peaks. Especially, as seen from the sea, you literally never see anything like a plain or an elevated plateau; nothing corresponding to a prairie or pampas exists within it. There are interspersed all through it, and extending up the coves from the coast, low-lying fields and valleys, on which rice and other peculiar crops are grown. All through these, trenches and ditches run, bringing the water from the hills, which irrigate the crops. Japan thus presents the most anomalous contrast of a country at once low and swampy, and of course malarial, with a scenic effect of mountainous diversification and beauty such as in America we can scarcely conceive of. Much of the country, indeed, the most of it, would seem, but for the timber, quite worthless for the support of a population; and yet 40,000,000 people (though living mostly on rice and fish, of which latter the streams and seas abound with countless varieties, and wearing the cheapest and often the scantiest clothing) manage to subsist.

This Shimonoseki has about 25,000 people; and four miles up the coast is the fascinating town of Chofu, a quaint old *Samurai* town of 8,000 people, full of rather aristocratic Japanese homes, many of them surrounded by sun-dried cement yellow walls, with lovely gardens filled with persimmon trees, just now heavy with their autumn fruit.

We put in a busy day yesterday, going in jinrikishas out to Chofu in the morning, looking over everything, buying a few curios, returning in the rain, having a good dinner, a chatty afternoon, and closing up, at 10 o'clock last night, with another of those heavenly little prayer meetings, which I have enjoyed with so many circles in my nearly six weeks in Japan. All these dear workers seem very happy in their work, and bravely do they hold on to it, amid trials and privations of which we have little conception at home.

Mrs. Halsey and her little four-year-old child stayed alone, the only foreigners in the place, during a time when cholera was at its worst, while Mr. Halsey was away, overseeing the condition of the little groups of believers in the out-towns; but not a fear did she intimate to me, and not a whine have I heard. They rather live in a high degree of enthusiasm over the privilege of thus serving the Japanese for Christ's sake.

This morning, we were all up at 6 o'clock to get me off by the steamer from Kobe. Brothers Halsey and Shoemaker came with me by the sampan (native boat) across the strait half a mile to meet the steamer. The steamer lay to for half an hour. We talked fast till the signal struck; then the two Morgan Park fellows and the gentle English sister descended the steps into the mail launch, and, waving their hats and handkerchiefs, they passed, I thought, rather sadly away toward the Shimonoseki landing. Above the landing on a high hill, reached by 140 stone steps, in a long, low bungalow, the Halseys live. The house was in full view, touched by the glory of the sun just rising over the eastern mountains; and the two other ladies and the sweet child, who, I was told, prayed very earnestly for me last night — (a rare thing it is for a new American face to be seen in that home, and there is absolutely no other white child with whom she can play) could be discerned waving farewells from the long white veranda. Thus, with a new sense of the renunciation involved in giving the gospel to the heathen, I breathed a fervent, "God bless them, and multiply a hundred-fold their reward." The fact that this work is not in vain, was emphasized anew as I caught a view of the roof of the disused heathen temple, half-way down the hill, in front of the mission compound, in which the little church at Shimonoseki of fifty members now regularly worships, having rented it from the priests.

Thus idolatry is slowly but surely being dispossessed. All day long I have been casting glances backward to those enchanted shores, made sacred and forevermore a part of my own life from the character of my peculiar embassage to them; and I have prayed, as I never could have done before, for Japan's redemption, and that the nearly forty of our own dear workers whom I have met, sympathized and prayed with, and — if I may give their word for it — encouraged, may have a large share in it.

Nay, more: I have thought again and again of the relations of other shores to these, and I have coveted for the luxuriously living, exalted American Baptists a consecration of men and money to this land's renovation, of which we have not yet conceived. O America! rouse thee to this work, and join our prayers! Pastors of our myriad churches, prove yourselves worthy brethren of those whose yearning eyes followed our departing steamer to-day, as if saying, " We, too, would join you on the journey homeward, were our lives our own." For " Truly, if they had been mindful of that country from whence they came out, they might have had opportunity to have returned."

Nagasaki.

This most westerly treaty port, a city of some 60,000 souls, the great port of the rich and populous island of Kiu Shiu, is as yet without a Baptist

PAPPENBERG. APPROACH TO NAGASAKI.

missionary. We have here, however, an earnest brother, Professor L. E. Martin, a graduate of Kalamazoo College, who in March next will leave his government school work, and, with his three years' experience in the country and good start in the language, will enter our mission service, and open a station at some inland point in this island, probably at Kurume.*

We arrived last night, and are spending the Sabbath here. Several missionary brethren met us this morning, and took us ashore. We saw several missions of the Presbyterians, Methodists and others in flourishing activity. The harbor is fine, and the scenery very picturesque. Just at the entrance to the harbor, we passed the historic little island of Pappenberg, from the cliffs of which so many thousands of Catholic martyrs were flung to their death about three centuries ago, when the Japanese rose up and exterminated the disciples of the early Jesuitical influence which followed upon Xavier's conquests.

* Since the above was penned, Brother Martin has married Dr. Clough's daughter, and gone to Ongole, India.

CHAPTER IV.

A Buddhist Doctrine of Justification by Faith.

AMONG the objects of most striking interest which the traveller sees in the ancient city of Kioto, Japan, are the "Temples of Hon-gwan-ji"—"Eastern" and "Western," so called. One of these temples is quite new: in fact, it is yet building. To those sanguine souls who are inclined to think that the force of idolatry in Japan is spent, that idolatrous shrines generally are in the last stages of decay, and that no more will be built, we commend a few facts concerning the present building of this new Hon-gwan-ji structure. It is built entirely from the free-will offerings of the people of the Buddhist sect which it represents, from all parts of the empire. These contributions are of costly jewels, metals, woods for the building, human hair, and money without stint.

On one of the platforms of the temple are twenty-four coils of rope from three to four inches in diameter, made of this human hair. Attached to one of the coils is a placard with this inscription : —

"Since the thirteenth year of Meji (1880), when the rebuilding of the two halls of the Eastern Hon-gwan-ji was begun, the faithful laymen and laywomen of every place have been unanimous in presenting to the principal temple, Hon-gwan-ji, strong ropes made of their own hair, to be used for the work of erection. The number of these ropes reached fifty-three. Twenty-nine of them became worthless from use. The total length of the remaining twenty-four is 4,528 feet, and the total weight is 11,567 pounds."

Besides these ropes were several large coils of hair, some of them gray, the gifts of the aged, which came in too late to admit of being used. The total cost of this temple is to reach the sum of several millions of dollars. The offerings of devotees in Kioto, apart from gifts for erecting the temple, to these two shrines, during the year 1889, amounted to the sum of $367,000. And yet most of the contributions were from people who are extremely poor. Out of Kioto's population of nearly 500,000, less than 500 people pay a tax amounting to $15, so poor are they.

Magnificent, however, as the temple is, and regal as the offerings were, the peculiarities of the sect whose primal shrine is here are of far more interest to me.

These people are a sect of the Buddhists, but they represent a departure from pure ancient Buddhism of rare significance. They worship Buddha, indeed, but him only in the character of Amita, or Amitabha, whom they conceive to be the idealization and glorification of highest discipleship to the primitive Buddha. They eschew all works of merit; they depend on the absolute, unconditioned mercy of Amita; they have a doctrine of justification by faith only, apart from meritorious deeds; their priests are not celibates nor ascetics; they carry on active and aggressive missionary operations, and to this end they highly educate their young priests, sending some of them to the Doshisha Congregational College in Kioto, and even to Oxford, England. Three hundred of these neophytes are gathered in one school near their chief Kioto temples.

They base their doctrine on that portion of the Buddhist Scripture known as the "Sam-bu-Kio," in which is recorded the peculiar vow made by Amitabha that he would "accept Buddhaship, but under the condition that salvation was made attainable by all who should sincerely desire to be born into Buddha's kingdom, and should signify their desire by invoking his name ten times." This vow is called the "Former, or Real Vow," and hence the name given to the two great temples in Kioto, "Hon-gwan-ji," meaning "Temple of the Real Vow," referring to their basal doctrine.

This sect is now divided really into two — the one known as the "Jodo" sect and the other as the "Shin Shiu."

Originally they were one, taking their rise in the beginning of the twelfth century under a great teacher, known as Honen Shonin. This man was enough in earnest to break with earlier Buddhists, and to outline a doctrine far in advance of Buddha's in some respects. He taught the worship of Amita, and also the doctrine of justification by faith in Amita's boundless mercy; but he also urged the value of meritorious deeds, and insisted on the cardinal idea of Buddhism, that no help can be expected in the conquest of passions outside of one's self. It was at this point that there sprang up, early in the thirteenth century, a departure from the teaching of the Jodo sect.

The Shin Shiu sect differs from the Jodo sect in its teaching at the following points. First, it holds that salvation is due to faith only in the power and willingness of Amita to save mankind, and that the invocation implied in the Real Vow is to be used only as an act of thanksgiving, and not as an act of merit for mercy received; secondly, that this salvation is received at once, and not at death, and that the believer is taken thenceforth under Amita's merciful protection; thirdly, that morality is of equal importance with faith; fourthly, that while Nirvana, or eternal happiness, is to be attained (as all Buddhists teach) by the extinction of the passions through many deaths and re-births, yet this extinction of passions (contrary to the usual Buddhist teaching) may be reached through help from another — that is, from Amitabha, he being the chief of the Buddhas. The name "Amitabha" signifies "boundless life" or "immeasurable light."

The Shin Shius maintain that their rival sect, the Jodos, have departed from the former and true teaching at these several points. The Shin Shius have undertaken to restore the true teaching respecting the "Former Vow." Hence they are sometimes called the Protestants of Japanese Buddhism. The proportions to which this sect of reformers has grown are remarkable. They have in all Japan 18,000 temples and shrines, and are accounted the wealthiest and most powerful of all the sects. They possess no fixed properties which might be considered endowments, but depend entirely on the offerings of the people for support and for purposes of propagandism. They actively undertake missions abroad, especially in Corea and China.

The creed runs as follows: "Rejecting all religious austerities and other action, giving up all idea of self-power, we rely upon Amita Buddha with the whole heart for our salvation in the future life, which is the most important thing, believing that at the moment of putting our faith in Amita Buddha our salvation is settled. From that moment invocation of his name is observed as an expression of gratitude and thankfulness for Buddha's mercy. Moreover, being thankful for the reception of this doctrine from the founder and succeeding chief priests, whose teachings were so benevolent, and as welcome as light in a dark night, we must also keep the laws which are fixed for our duty during our whole life."

A most extraordinary statement this, to proceed from men presumably destitute of revelation. Substitute for Amita Buddha, here conceived of as the chief of the Buddhas, the name of our Lord Jesus Christ, and you have substantially the New Testament doctrine of justification by faith as amplified by Paul in the Epistles to the Romans and Galatians.

A still more modern statement of the belief of this remarkable sect is given by Mr. Akamatsu, a distinguished member of the sect in Kioto, and published in the April number, for 1881, of the *Chrysanthemum*, now discontinued.

Says Mr. Akamatsu: "Amita Buddha always exercises his boundless mercy upon all creatures, and shows a great desire to help and influence all people who rely upon him to complete all merits, and to be reborn into Paradise. Our sect pays no attention to other Buddhas, but, putting faith only in the great desire of Amita Buddha, expects to escape from the miserable world, and to enter into Paradise in the next life. From the time of putting faith in the saving power of Buddha, we do not need any power of self-help, but need only to keep his mercy in heart, and invoke his name in order to remember him. These doings we call 'thanksgiving for salvation.'"

Is this an uninstructed groping for "the grace of God which bringeth salvation," which is accurately and specifically met in Paul's great expositions? Is this an ignorant worship of the essential Christ under the phrase of Amita Buddha?

We would not dare say that these doctrinal conceptions, purely considered, are generally entertained by the adherents of the sect, much less that they have popular power to bring spiritual rest and the sense of salvation to the mass of devotees!

How shall we account for the existence of the conceptions at all in any measure, by even a single mind? Shall it be on the ground that "He hath not left himself without a witness among any nation"? Whether we account for it or not, what a prepared soil is here, in the providence of God, for such missionary endeavor as shall be able to go in among such a people and explain to them the real way of God more perfectly! What an evangelizing oracle the Epistle of Paul to the Romans would prove in meeting this unique state of heathen mind! May God raise up and bring some man to the Kingdom of the Sunrise for such a time as this!

CHAPTER V.

In the Chinese Empire.

Arrival at Shanghai.

SHANGHAI, October 22.

RISING at daybreak on the morning of the third day out from Nagasaki, Japan's most westerly seaport, we find that we are passing the "Saddle Islands." During the night the sea has turned from its usual deep green to a dull yellow, and by noontide it is a huge swash of ochre-colored waves. We are told that we have entered into the mouth of the great Yang Tse River, which, in its mighty flow, carries forevermore the yellow sands of the vast lands through which it flows, a full 100 miles out into the sea. This river is the fourth largest in the world; and its delta, of over seventy-five miles long and in places over forty miles wide, is year by year extending. That long, low-lying dark line which lies on the water yonder on our port side, which one could easily mistake for a shadow, is the first land which salutes us as we head on towards Shanghai. An hour or two later, we discern the outlines of the old walled town of Woosung, with a quaint adobe or mud-colored old fort on our right. We anchor a half-hour for the tide to so rise that we can cross the bar. At this point we leave the arm of the Yang Tse up which we have been sailing, and enter the Woosung River, sailing up the stream on a graceful curve for twelve miles to Shanghai.

We move on between the low, flat, uninteresting shores, in such melancholy contrast to the ever picturesque lofty shores of Japan; having become accustomed to those for some six weeks past, we confess to being spoiled for most coast scenery.

"Look," says a companion at my right, "at those three full-rigged, graceful brigs," following each other like a naval column, making their way under escort of tugs out to sea. "And see! they each float the stars and stripes of America!" and a few moments later, as they meet and glide past us, graceful, silent and queenly as swans, gilded by the western sunset, our hearts glow afresh towards the far-off home which our country's flag brings near to us.

On we go; and now the great black forms of sea-going steamers — German, English, French, Chinese and Japanese — begin to fill the stream. Among them, on our left, are two men-of-war, evidently new, flashing with the jet black of their hulls, rigged to perfection, brilliant signals flying from the top-gallants. Half-way up the main and mizzen masts is a sort of turret or round tower of iron, from which, in the event of being captured and boarded, a few daring men might fight with desperation, and virtually clear the decks of a capturing force. We are told that these glistening new war ships, equipped with the best of cannon, as complete as they can be made, are only specimens of a numerous and constantly growing war fleet, which some near day will compel to a reckoning those western nations, including our own, which with impunity are smiting China in the face.

THE GREAT WALL.

What are those numerous small hayrick-looking piles which we see yonder over the shore line, filling square miles of low flat lands, as if they were a huge harvest-field of haymakers on the flat lands of Northern Indiana? "Ah," says an old China missionary at my left, "that is indeed a harvest-field, but not of the sweet new-mown hay of America. The reaper's name who holds carnival there is Death; and those huge mounds, without a slab, are graves; and they are piled so large and high in a kind of rivalry, which the people exercise to emphasize the degree of honor which they bestow on their dead ancestors." The names of the dead are inscribed on tablets, kept on the god-shelf at the people's homes; and these, in ever-increasing numbers, are the gods they chiefly worship.

The vestibule to China through which we are passing is, then, a vestibule of death; loathsome, made revolting in the extreme, because all about and among those mounds, and on the river banks as we move on, we see, not merely well-shaped mounds, but numerous bare, unburied coffins, covered over only with a matting of reeds, because the friends of the dead are, in numerous cases, too poor to bury them at all; and so the coffins lie there as if dropped on the way to burial, to fester in the sun and breed a malaria which, no wonder, often amounts to wide-spread pestilence. If this be one of the forecourts of China, what must the interior be? If romance be the constraining motive of a new missionary to China, it will begin to perish here. If, however, he knows in his own soul the power of Christ's resurrection, and is on fire with a divine fuel to impart Christ's vitality

NEW SHANGHAI.

to a people lying more putrid than was Lazarus in his rock chamber, this corridor of death through which the missionary passes up the Woosung River will nerve him to declare "Jesus and the resurrection," as many heroes have done before him, through the great cities of this sepulchre empire till the whole land shall know their power, and the shadow of death shall be turned into the morning.

The "Empire Brewery," in its solid stone buildings on the right bank, looks as if it did not

46 *In Brightest Asia.*

CITY GATE, SHANGHAI.

doubt its call to China. It evidently has come to stay. Those two great yellow opium hulks, floating there like cobras with deadly fangs, basking in the sunset glow, have no thought of retreating. They seem to have no impatience, waiting there for registry. They can wait for any length of time, and seem to say, " We'll get in our work yet, and never you mind. Don't you see a kind of first-fruit of our harvest down the river yonder? We are the mound-builders of the present age; not the age of stone, but of stony hearts. Some of those great temples of commerce yonder, in the English concession, beautiful and sumptuous as the palaces of Venice, sitting enthroned like hers, on thronged canals, behind the park, on the Bund, vibrant with the strains of an English band, are the product and the apparatus of our game of death. That makes our game respectable, and we count that an offset to the ghastly mound-building down the river." Aye! and along all the rivers, and over all the hillsides of poor opium-demented, mammon-cursed China.

OLD NORTH GATE, SHANGHAI.

Our vessel — the " Yokohama Maru " — sidles up to her moorings. John Chinaman has come out by the thousand to see us land, and to pick up a few " cash " from the newly arrived " foreign saints." A dozen of our countrymen, bronzed, and some gray in the service, are seen among the throng to welcome the meagre reinforcement to their mission stations, which, thank God, the autumn steamers do usually bring. No representative of the American Baptist Missionary Union, alas! is there. A Presbyterian sister, who stands at my side, and whose home is here, asks: " Do you see that tall, serene-faced, calm man, who stands with arms folded (while the whole throng is a-howl with Chinese voices), in native costume and cue? That is Mr. Herring, of the Southern Baptist Board. We call him ' Our Mr. Herring.' We all claim him. He's so nice!" A few moments more, and he comes on board, commissioned by Mr. Goddard of Ningpo to meet me; a " rikisha " is called, and, bag and baggage, I am taken as a brother to his own home, near the " Old North Gate " of the wall of the native city. Here stands the mission-house built and occupied for nearly forty years by the lamented Dr. Yates. Alongside of it now is another, occupied by the *Companion* missionary, Brother Tatum; while just near the corner, opposite, is the substantial stone chapel, long used by the devoted missionaries at this post.

The evening tea over, the chapel bell began its call to worshippers. Brother Herring was to have a service, " not of the church at all," he said, " but for outsiders — the heathen — for whomsoever may come — a service we have three times weekly." Tired as I was from the voyage and the excitement of six busy weeks in Japan, I resolved, on that first night on the shores of China, to see what kind of a service this would be. We went to the chapel. A simple hymn was sung, a few people at a time coming in as we sang, until forty-five persons, men and women — some smoking pipes — came in, crowding to the front seats; and then our dear brother, taking the great commission for a text, proceeded to talk to those poor souls with fluency and warmth, in a winning, smiling, tender way, that even though, as in my case, not a word was understood, would have convinced a sphinx that he had the greatest and divinest message on earth to tell. It is an inspiration to hear a man, after being only five years in a country, stand up and preach to a people in their own tongue, like a native, and for a half-hour to observe him winning on his congregation at every stroke. To me, I confess also, that it was no drawback that he spoke with the Chinese cap on, with the long braid down his back, especially as I considered that his hearers saw in him a representative of Christ; a man at one with themselves, both in inward sympathy and outward form.

I heard of a young woman in Minnesota, a sister of one of our missionaries in China, who, when she saw a photograph of her brother in his Chinese costume, almost fainted. Some said, "Cruel!" Knowing the spirit of men like these, I have been led to think otherwise. How think ye God the Father's heart must have fainted — aye, broke! when He saw His only begotten Son in garb of our human race? There certainly is no merit or value in any outward dress for its own sake; but if for Christ's sake and love of the heathen, and increased ability to get near them, it be worn, what then? Is not "Wisdom justified of her children?"

Following Brother Herring's talk, a big square-rigged Chinese brother — pastor of the mission at Soo Chow, one of seven choice men trained by Dr. Yates — rose, and gave us twenty minutes more in a similar vein. I cannot say which used the better Chinese. I am sure they were each *en rapport* with the other and with their hearers. Thus ended my first evening in China, and I am ready for more of the same sort.

Shanghai as a Base of Operations.

Pending my trip up the Yang Tse, I found opportunity to look into the many-sided work of other societies than our own. My first introduction, as I have intimated, was to the work of our Southern brethren. Stations have been established at Hangchow, Soo Chow and Ching Kiang, as well as at Shanghai.

Dr. Yates was the pioneer of this mission, a North Carolina man; and five of the families out of the six now working in the mission were recruited from North Carolina. Dr. Yates labored here for forty years, and left behind him a stable church of some seventy members, several well-trained native preachers, and the beginnings of work in the out-stations named. His contributions to the literature of Chinese missions were considerable, and of a high quality.

One of the notable trophies of Dr. Yates' work is a character known as Deacon Wang. This man was an early convert, and by many years of consistent living he has proved his genuine devotion to Christ. At the time of his conversion, he was a rice dealer. He was at once met with the question whether he should observe the Sabbath. This is one of the crucial questions to a Chinaman, to whom all days of the week are alike equally profane. He came to the missionary for counsel. He, of course, could give him but one direction: "Close up your shop on Saturday night. Put upon your door, 'Rest day'; come to-morrow.'"

Wang hesitated and struggled. He knew he would lose trade, for a time at least. He however decided rightly. For a time, of course, his customers fell off. Some derided him, but he persevered, even though he lost much, and came into straits. Finally, however, the scales began to turn; his strict honesty and consistency had gained him confidence with country dealers who came in along the canals, bringing boatloads of their rice for sale. In time these dealers, arriving Saturday night at market, were willing to wait over till Monday for the sake of dealing with Wang, because they knew his quotation of prices would be so fair and his honor was without challenge. This good name soon brought great prosperity, and Wang became rich. He at length retired from business with a competence. He has contributed largely to missions.

A few years since he bought in the old city of Shanghai some land, and built thereon a commodious chapel, all at his own expense; and for years he has himself preached there week-days and Sundays to multitudes of his countrymen. He is now an old man. His large and imposing presence in the church last Sunday impressed me deeply before I knew who he was. In the afternoon I went to hear him in his own chapel. How his face beamed behind his great eyeglasses with tortoise-shell bows, as he both preached and sang the redemption story! The Chinaman can be Christianized, and become likewise a chosen vessel to others. Wang is the demonstration.

Next to the missions of our Southern brethren, I was desirous of seeing the headquarters of the China Inland Mission, also in Shanghai. I had heard in America of the splendid new building, the gift of the friends, and in part of the missionaries themselves, of this mission. I was scarcely prepared to see so ample and fine accommodations, and such a beehive of varied activities.

HEADQUARTERS CHINA INLAND MISSION.

The buildings stand on three sides of a large quadrangle. Along the front are several mission-houses, built in a row, some three stories in height. In the centre is a spacious hall for public meetings. Here, also, a prayer meeting is held weekly on Saturday nights. On one side of the quadrangle, facing inward, is a row of apartments, including parlors, dining-rooms, offices, mailing and shipping rooms, etc., with conveniences for the temporary living and lodgment of some forty missionaries in transit to and from their stations, or who may come in for periodic rest. On a third side of the quadrangle are rooms for the temporary accommodation of native workers who may come in from time to time. Here they can board themselves, doing their own cooking,

STREET IN SHANGHAI.

spreading their mats, etc. The whole establishment looks like business, I assure you. I received most cordial attention from Mr. Stevenson, the deputy superintendent in charge, and other missionaries, and found I was there not wholly unknown, from my relations to Dr. Guinness, and from my articles in *Regions Beyond*.

When you add to the facilities here reared two training-schools for all new arrivals,— one for men at Gan King, and one for women at Yang Chow,— and also at Chefoo, in Northern China, a first-class boarding-school for their own children, also largely patronized by English civil-service people, you will see that this is a most thorough-going institution.

Those who suppose that this mission is ephemeral or lacks organization, are greatly misled. That God's blessing is signally upon it also, especially as a pioneering agency in opening up the interior places, is beyond a doubt. For example, we Baptists have supposed we were doing a heroic thing in placing in Szchuen two missionaries; the C. I. M. have in that same province forty-seven. True, some of their most excellent workers are inclining to come, after a season, into relation to our denominational boards. This, too, is well, both for them and us.

Still other societies have strong agencies in Shanghai, such as the London Missionary Society, with its veteran

CHINESE CARRIAGE.

MISSIONARIES, EASTERN CHINA.

representative, Mr. Muirhead, pastor over a large flock, and, though having reached fourscore years, still evangelizing with ardor and power. Then there is the work of the American Congregationalists and the Presbyterians, with their great and influential press and their large schools and hospitals; the college of the American Methodists, under Dr. Allen — the Jupiter Tonans as an advocate of high views of educational agencies to the higher classes if we are ever to convert China. The Church Missionary Society is here in force. A great cathedral adorns one of the finest squares in the English concession. The Seventh Day Adventists, with schools and a hospital, are scarcely behind any. The Bible societies, both British and American, are eminently aggressive and successful, selling through their numerous colporters hundreds of thousands of Bibles annually for hard Chinese cash.

With all these varied agencies, Shanghai would seem verily a modern Antioch of strategic influence for the spread of the gospel through the "Middle Kingdom."

May the Spirit of all power give the gospel wing!

JUNK, INLAND SEA.

CHAPTER VI.

The Eastern China Mission.

A Foot-Boat Trip.

Inland 60 Miles from Ningpo, Oct. 24, 1890.

IF you could now take me in in your vision, you would think I had reached heathendom indeed. I am trying to write sitting in the bottom of my boat,—a boat about sixteen feet long and four feet wide, covered with several sections of mats bent over bamboo bows, to protect from sun and weather. My baggage and bedding, and a few conveniences for our workers living up the river, fill a part of the boat. My bunk of comforters occupies the centre, on which I sit; and at the stern, on a high seat, is my boatman, propelling with his feet the cylinder-shaped craft, tapering at each end. There the fellow sits bolt upright; and with both feet on the handle of the oar, so arranged that the feet will not slip off, he manages, by a deft use of his legs, acquired through much practice, to put the whole strength of his limbs, and body as well, on that oar. Then, in order that the boat may not swing around, he carries a paddle under his right arm, with which he steers the craft. Nor is this all of the ingenious man's accomplishments. When he desires to make time (for these *Push*man cars of the Celestials rarely stop for refreshments), having both hands free, he is able to sit there, and, with his bowl of rice and chopsticks, take his dinner, while with his feet he diligently pushes away as if turning a crank. My companion, Brother Goddard, has another craft of the same kind, except that his being a little larger, we call it the grand saloon, and at meal-times I draw up alongside, and by a careful movement— which, if not well managed, may upset both boats — I jump into his boat, and we take our meals together. He is an "old hand" at this kind of travel, and has the completest outfit of dishes and equipments of all sorts with which to do it well.

FOOT-BOAT.

We are off for Shaohing, 100 miles inland, to visit Mr. and Mrs. Jenkins, and also Brother Adams, who has come in from Kinhwa, 200 miles farther on, in order to meet us. It is a novel trip, I assure you, and full of interest. We are moving through a great plain of ten miles or so in width, through which canals run in a great net-work; and away on each side stretch low ranges of barren mountains. Villages fill the region, and line the banks of these canals at

WAYSIDE INN.

intervals. Boats loaded with cotton, wood and bamboo, and journeying people, are coming and going. We are just now passing a heathen Buddhist temple, marked by the reddish paint which sparsely covers it, as well as by its size and quality — far superior to the poor, squalid and dreary-looking homes, if homes they can be called. This temple is only one of scores we are passing all day long.

This morning about 7 o'clock, we drew up at the landing of a considerable town to rest our boatman a little, and while waiting walked out into the town and visited the little Presbyterian chapel. A poor sort of a chapel we should call it — not more expensive than a good woodhouse at home, with nothing for the people to sit on but rude benches, like saw-horses, without backs; and it was very small, seating perhaps thirty persons. The thing itself would have been contemptible as a building in my eyes, but for what I saw in three persons in connection with it. The first was a bright old man near the landing as we came off the boat, who showed us the way with evident pride, and who at once had recognized Mr. Goddard as the "Jesus-doctrine-man." The next was an old woman, looking feeble and forlorn, who, in response to a subsequent inquiry of Mr. Goddard's as to the location of the chapel, at once, with an explosive exclamation, as if we had touched powder with a torch, nodded assent, clapped her hands upon her breast, and saying,—in Chinese, of course,—"I am a member of that church!" started off on a trot to show us the place. Arriving there, she rattled away at the doors and windows of the house of the native elder who is in charge, until she brought him out. We went in and sat down; and shortly the elder, with a handsome face, in clean clothing and so bright an eye, came in, ordered the usual tea to be brought, and he and Mr. Goddard had a chat about the good work. If I had seen in China nothing but the scene of this morning, though I have seen vastly more and higher manifestations of transforming influence, I should say that this work is not in vain. Bear in mind that this place I have referred to is only one of the little out-stations of a score or two of churches in this immediate district. Mr. Goddard read for me the text which hung behind the pulpit, "For there is one God and one Mediator, Jesus Christ." If there were nothing but that there, it continually preaches what this great people need to know.

A Ningpo Household.

You are wondering how about Miss Inveen, Miss Corbin and Miss Stewart, who are such important factors in the work there, and among whom your own dear Miss Parker is so soon to begin work. Well, there they are, as busy as bees, and as happy as possible, I judge, in the good work that appears to absorb them. I am witness to it, for yesterday I sat at their dinner table in the house which Dr. Lord (while consul) built at a cost of $5,000, and then at his death turned over, with other valuable property, to the Missionary Union. You may recall that Miss Corbin came from the church of which I was first pastor, in Rockford, Ill. Miss Inveen I had met and heard speak in Minnesota. It did seem like a dream to find myself now really among them in China! Of course we talked up all the dear Minnesota people and the churches we had severally loved there; and with a fine photograph of "Uncle Boston" and his family in a group hanging on the wall, smiling down on us so genially, it did seem as if we were all children again in our gladness. We could almost hear Uncle Boston say: "Now, boys and girls, if you'll keep still long enough, I'll tell you a story." Well, it was a Minnesota day, in the course of which the Western China Mission and the coming reinforcements due by the next steamer, "The China," etc., all came in for glowing comment. It did seem a pity we couldn't have Miss Parker (so soon to arrive) with us, but I hope yet to greet her on her arrival at Shanghai. I have at least witnessed the home in which she is to live, the promising school of girls in which she will begin to teach, the women's school, the hospital, the boys' school, in all of which she will find deep interest, and I have seen the people living there within the hoary battlemented walls of a heathen city, which will move her heart to a compassion such as no scene she ever looked upon before has awakened. I am now visiting the outlying native churches and fields with which she will become helpfully familiar. May God brace her for what she is to meet,—a moral darkness and dearth that can be felt.

Shaohing. October 28.

Mr. Goddard and I are to-day on the return trip from Shaohing. We have had five days of it out on this route, and it will take to-day and to-night besides to bring us back to Ningpo. We

LEANING PAGODA AT NINGPO.

stopped with Mr. and Mrs. Jenkins at Shaohing. They have been thirty years in this region, and they are vigorous still, and working away with unabated zeal. Mr. J. has, besides his evangelistic work in several stations, a training-school for preachers, having seven students with him at present. Mr. Adams and his eleven-year-old son, Arthur, came in from Kinhwa, and we all had a great visit together. Mr. Adams was one of Dr. Guinness' first students, was several years with the C. I. M. in Bhamo, Burma, and also with that mission in China for one year. He joined our mission about eight years ago, and has proved one of our very best workers, having built up good strong stations all about him.

On Sunday afternoon, he, Mr. Goddard and I started out through the city to visit two or three of the native preaching-places — little, cheaply fitted up sheds of affairs, with a clay floor, and a few rude seats like saw-horses. We needed no church bell or other attractions than our sensational selves. For attracting a crowd in a real wild Chinese town or city, nothing can surpass a procession of three foreigners. We had a train equal to that of small boys which streams after one of Buffalo Bill's Wild West shows, only our crowd was made up of men, women and boys; and with exclamations of all sorts they were commenting on our ridiculousness of hats, shoes, coats, neckties, etc. As we reached chapel after chapel,— even though, as in one case, the meeting had not begun, or as in another, though the meeting had closed and the doors also,— we had but to simply open them, walk in, turn around and begin. Our audience was there: we brought it with us; several of them. Several times, likewise, the audience changed while the meeting went on. They came and went without reference to pauses in the programme. We really came to the latter meeting to see the service and hear one of the students preach; but as he had finished, and we had our crowd, likewise two preachers of our own who knew Chinese as well as English, I set them at it,— first Goddard and then Adams. I could only silently pray, and I never felt more like it in my life, as these two earnest and tactful brethren poured the truth into them. Many gave good attention. One big earnest fellow interrupted, saying, "What you say is true enough, but we are unable to do the thing you require." This gave Brother Goddard a new opportunity to nail his audience to a fresh attention by explaining what grace enables the sinner to do. Brother Adams got hold of the children especially, a dozen of whom stood up before him, and took his simply illustrated points as keenly as one of "Uncle Boston's" meetings would, and with as much roguish twinkle in the eyes. These ten-minute sermonettes, composed on the spot, being ended, Brother Adams got out a bundle of tracts, which were taken like hot-cakes, and we went on our way, never to meet those souls again till the judgment, but thankful for even this slight contact with them. But oh, they are so wretched in their moral disease and swinishness; and they love it, for aught I can see, just as tenaciously as the civilized millionnaire at home loves his environment.

Going up and down these rivers and canals, lined on both sides with numberless villages, surrounded by the yellow rice-fields, villages in which the bronzed, blue-calico clothed (rather ragged than clothed), hatless distortions and monstrosities of humanity swarm, I have seen much to move the heart. Rooted in their ages of inherited bias, vice and animalism, filled with a mass of superstition which religiously forbids change even of the most worthless or injurious things about them (like, e. g., the removal of an old rotting boat hulk from a canal channel), or even to rescue a companion from drowning, lest they should offend their Fung Shway, or spirit of good luck, and thus awaken his ill will and bring on dire calamities, how shall they ever be rescued from such a state? Surely only the power of a supernatural gospel can reach them. And yet most potential beginnings are made, and we cannot doubt that the long nightmare of ages is about to vanish. China is late in waking, but wake she must and will.

A Noted Tomb.

While at Shaohing we made a pilgrimage to the tomb of Yü the Great, with whom authentic Chinese history begins. He lived 2200 years B. C. Noah's period was 2800 B. C. This is the oldest historic tomb on earth! There is an image representative of the old fellow — Sinim's emperor — and also of several of his courtiers about him, and an old temple of remarkably fine architectural features on the spot. We didn't see any of his bones, nor get any locks of his hair, nor a tooth; but we are sure that this sanctuary marks the burial-place of a monarch older even than Rameses of Egypt — older than Abraham.

TOMB OF YÜ, THE GREAT — GREAT-GRANDSON OF NOAH.

Leaving the tomb, we ascended also a famous mountain which overlooks the spot, — one of myriad peaks of the mountain range lying away to the southwest. It was a tough climb, right up 1,500 feet to a crag of frightfully small proportions which caps the summit, and on which stands a Buddhist temple, called the Temple of the Holy Incense Pot. But what a view rewarded our climb! On the southwest a mountain range of great variety of form, with numberless cosey coves and terraced slopes, ripe with harvests nestling in the long narrow defiles. Away to the east the Hang Chow Bay, an arm of the sea, say twenty miles distant, makes into the land, over which a hazy mist is floating. A vast plain stretches out on all sides northward as far as the eye can reach, fairly golden with waving rice harvests. Through and through this mighty plain run canals in an intricate net-work, the lines of which, glancing silvern in the sunlight, cannot be counted for number. They out-Holland Holland. There are literally no roads except the paths on the canal banks. All traffic is conveyed by boats only. Never a wagon is seen, nor a horse; occasionally a buffalo or a bullock hauls a load. Trees stud the plain, and sometimes adorn the canal banks. These now are dressed in autumn tints; only instead of our maple, the brilliant foliage is that of the tallow tree. From the berries of this tree the natives actually obtain a vegetable tallow from which they make their candles. The trees not standing on the canals usually mark tombs, and of these the whole district possesses a multitude. The mountain-sides are embossed with hillocks and mounds wherein for 4,000 years these descendants of the great Yü have been laid in common dust with their still mortal though vaunted monarch.

Still keeping in mind our landscape, we see rising sheer out of the great flat plain in occasional districts a great isolated mountain form, bold and precipitous, like those about Edinburgh, giving a touch of majesty to all. Scattered throughout the whole scene, and to be numbered only by the hundreds, are cities, towns and villages wherein dwell actually an aggregate of millions of human souls. The walls of the houses are white; the tiled roofs are uniformly black.

In every city and town your eye takes in, you can discern the always conspicuous red or yellow walls of a building which is sure to be a temple or ancestral hall, in which the idolatry of the place stalks ghastly and grim as death itself. The dust of ages and the filth of birds fill all the shrines; the mould of damp is rotting the very fibre of the wooden images or corroding those of brass; the squeaks of bats by the thousand are heard among the cornices and in the interstices of the elaborate framing of the richly decorated but rotting rafters; and death and doom are in and through and on the whole satanic fabric. Here on this mount, as on another Mount Carmel, for us four missionaries of the cross, with this vast panorama before us, was a place for prayer. Never again on that spot should we four thus meet. We felt the challenge rising to us from the plain, vocal with the woes of heathenism, and reiterated from the priests of Baal who, in the temple on the summit hard by us, hoodwink the deluded myriads that annually flock to this high place. Shall Baal thus forever triumph? It cannot, must not be. So there we uncover, and two of our number, appealing once more to the Lord God of Elijah, plead that God may speedily among our score or more of flocklets in the East China Mission — from Ningpo to Kinhwa — answer by fire, and prove that He is God. It was a high hour in our lives on that October day. With heaven to witness, with bending angels listening near, with the whole mountain filled, we doubt not, with the chariots and horsemen of the true God, our prayer at least was registered in behalf of the souls dwelling in that vast and beautiful Shaohing plain. It was something to have looked upon them from that mount, and to at least have wept over them for Jesus' sake. May God give the tongues of fire to preach to them, and win them to Jesus' love, and that right speedily!

CHAPTER VII.

Up the Yang-tse-Kiang.

Visit to Nanking.

November 7.

UP the Yang-tse River a day and a night's sail by steamer, on the left bank, stands the historic old city of Nanking. It was the capital of the Chinese empire, under the Ming dynasty from 1368 to 1644; and in some sense it is the southern capital still, a viceroy over three provinces having his official seat there. From our schoolboy days we had contracted a sentimental interest in the city of the famous Porcelain Tower, now, alas! completely effaced by the ravages incident to the Taiping War.

The history of this war being also fresh in mind, from a recent reading of the life of General Chinese Gordon and his connection therewith, had deepened our desire to see the place. We were therefore not slow to accept the invitation of two missionary friends whom we met in Shanghai, to go with them on their return to Nanking, the city of their labors.

We arrived at 4 o'clock in the morning; and while waiting for daylight, when we could engage small boats for transporting us up a canal five miles to the city gates, we had an experience of being huddled together with about 300 noisy, turbulent Chinese, on board the great landing-hulk.

For two hours we were in this babel, with nothing to do but to take in the scenes, listen to the hubbub over the distributions of baggage as it was put ashore, and absorb the smells. I had been led to think that because the Chinaman is constitutionally and from training a conservative, he was therefore a stolid and immobile sort of creature—a sphinx, in fact, who may sit and smile and smile, but who never breaks the silence if he can help it. But ah! miserable delusion! These Chinese in their native air, with nothing in the world to do but to walk off the plank of a steamer and to wait, each sitting on his luggage or taking a nap on the floor of the hulk, wrapped in his blanket, for two slow, drawling hours, were howling like dervishes, without a moment of let-up. For excitement and a generally rattled condition, they exceeded a Donnybrook fair or a stack of Kilkenny cats. If a fellow sang out an idea of any sort, a dozen voices would repeat it. Others would re-echo these. Any unlooked-for incident was the signal for a fresh outbreak. In an accident we are told the Chinaman loses his head sooner than a Frenchman. The Chinaman may be a conservative: but it is settled for us that in his native haunts he is never reserved, when there is half a chance to go off the handle.

At daybreak we are off up the canal, amid a perfect swarm of oared boats of every sort. These boats are as a rule unpainted; and when new and glistening with oil or varnish, finishing the handsome grained woods, junks though they are, they are by no means so rude or lumbering as we had preconceived them to be. Now and then a steam tug plies up or down the stream. Yonder is one coming, doubtless of English build, but native manned, and drawing behind it a train of three or four new yellow junks, from which the most brilliant red bunting is flying on all sides. From one mast-head floats the Dragon banner of the empire. This boat bears some army official.

The walls of the city now begin to appear, running in a long dark mass; now along the canal, then over a rocky promontory, and anon up over the hills into the far-away distance. These walls astonish us by their massiveness and height. The average height cannot be less than forty feet. They often rise to seventy-five and 100 feet. Including the filling of earth, they are forty feet in thickness. The outer shell is castellated. These walls enclose an area of not less than twenty-five miles around. In fact, the Nanking wall is the largest single enclosure in the world.

The first Ming monarch, Hung-Woo, who laid out and fortified this seat of empire, wrought a colossal thing. This wall, though having stood for 500 years, looks as if it were good for 2,500 years more, being in perfect repair. Of course it encloses more area than that required for the mere city itself. It embraces much of the open country adjacent, including rich agricultural lands, lakes, orchards, lofty hills and moors, on which pheasants and even the wild deer are often shot. This open country is very desolate and silent to an American eye. There is a sepulchral lonesomeness about its aspect and impress upon you. There is a sense of past generations departed since these hoary walls that lie on the horizon line yonder were builded. Indeed, the hillocks and mounds thrown up in such multitudes on all the slopes and across the plains force upon you afresh the reflection that China is one vast sepulchre, in which human beings of forty centuries lie entombed. Jerusalem itself could not impress one more with the sense of ancientness and generations gone forever. There are within the present walls the traces of two old cities within the modern city. One is known as "the Tartar City"; and the other is what was once known in Ming times as "the Forbidden or Imperial City." Both of these are now reduced to a waste, with occasional old bridges, beautiful in design, or the part of an old palace or royal road remaining.

The moats which skirted the division walls are filled up; and what were once rushing brooks running sparkling, clear, from the hills, are now dry ravines, with occasional slimy pools, sadly suggestive of the changed conditions.

An Army with Banners.

As we were passing through these dismantled remains of imperial pretensions of the past, we met a regiment of soldiers in single file, each with the traditional long, bannered lance, just entering the walls by the North Gate. They had been out to escort their officials to the temple of the Dragon King, beyond the Ming Tombs, that they might there pray for rain. It gave new reality to that Scripture phrase, "an army with banners"; but apart from the array of glaring red flags, I was amused at the pusillanimity of the force, with about as much discipline and form as a tribe of wild Comanche Indians, and as superstitious.

Since the Ming times, next to no progress has been made by the Chinese of Nanking. We were threading our way through ruins, due to war and its sad havocs, notably those of the Taiping Rebellion. It was in this city that the Tien Wang, or "Heavenly King," had his throne. Here the rebellion, after a two years' siege, collapsed, when the city was sacked and in a large part destroyed, even its beautiful and far-famed Porcelain Tower, and its people butchered wholesale, without mercy.

The Ming Tombs.

PORCELAIN TOWER, NANKING.

We were favored in having for our guide to the Ming Tombs Dr. Robert Beebe, of the American Methodist Episcopal Mission Hospital in Nanking. On three donkeys, each somewhat larger than a good-sized goat, three of us started out through the once forbidden city and the North Gate, over the grave-peopled hills, four miles to the northward. The remains of three elaborate structures are to be seen. The first is a sort of gateway consisting of three arches. A couple of hundred yards farther on, is the tomb of the younger Ming monarch. Directly over it is placed an immense turtle, carved from a single stone, which might weigh eight or ten tons; and rising from its back is a colossal slab of granite, fourteen feet in height, and about two feet by six in thickness and breadth, on which are inscriptions celebrating the achievements of the dynasty. Over all this are the ruined arches of a large stone building, eighty feet square, which is entered by four mammoth gateways, one on each side. Passing now to the westward, we find ourselves at the entrance of a long, curved roadway, leading for another mile to the tomb of the great Ming himself.

Colossal Images.

Along this roadway, at intervals of 100 yards or so, are colossal images in granite, of a peculiar character, and in pairs, facing each other from opposite sides of the way. First we pass through between two dogs standing; then between two kneeling; then between two pairs of tigers, then of lions, then of camels, then of huge elephants, then of horses, then of monumental pillars; then between two pairs each of military men, and of literati, then of more animals again, etc., for the distance of a full mile. We have now come around a large hill, in a circuitous way, Chinese superstition being much afraid of straight lines; and now passing over a bridge formed of triple arches abreast, we enter the ruins of what was once a temple gateway, then through a large court, over another stone bridge, and then up to the final court and arched entrance to the burial site itself.

The tomb of the great Ming is, as all Chinese tombs are, a hillock or miniature mountain, except that this is of vast size, only the rounding off of which can be artificial. The hill covers probably some six acres of ground at its base, and rises to perhaps 300 feet in height. On the top of this hill it is said the great ruler is buried. The whole hill is enclosed with a great wall about twenty feet in height and four feet in thickness. Just behind the entire artificial arrangements of which I have spoken, rises a great dragon-shaped mountain, called the Golden Pearly Mountain, purple with red sandstone and autumn herbage. The tomb hillock at its base was golden and scarlet with the tints of the autumn foliage. Indian summer haze gave atmosphere to all, and the scene was august with impressiveness and mystery.

GRANITE ANIMALS BEFORE MING TOMBS.

A Noble Type.

There stood with us there that day a brilliant young Chinaman, with flashing eye, in rich garb, secretary to the city yamen (or mayor), who had come to the spot to make preparations for the expected arrival, next day, of a great Tartar general, who had been sent from Pekin to represent the present emperor, in special prayer to the dead ancestral monarch. This young official explained to us the entire affair, and dilated at great length, and with eloquent gesticulation, on the grandeur of the sight, and the excellent arrangements of the "Fung Shway," admitting of the easy going and coming of the spirit of the mighty dead from and to his tomb. The young fellow, a Bismarck in proportions, fascinated us beyond measure. He was effusively polite and cordial. We could not but pray for the day when such specimens of China's young manhood, enlightened by the gospel and forsaking his superstitions, shall rise up, Luther-like, and stir this sleeping empire with Christ-like power.

Returning to the city, we made rapid visits to the several missions, all American, viz.: To the Methodist, with the large and influential Philander Smith Memorial Hospital, the boys' and girls' schools, chapels, etc.; to the Presbyterian, the Friends, and the Disciples' missions, all in flourishing conditions. We visited several of the noted temples, including the Confucian, second in rank only to the great one in Pekin.

We said farewell to our cordial host and guide for the day, and, wearied in body though filled with high appreciation of what we had seen, under escort of one of the Presbyterian mission servants, we passed out of the gate of the city just before it closed for the night, and by two boatmen were propelled in our houseboat, snugly sleeping, meanwhile, down to the landing, to catch the morning steamer to Hankow.

CHINESE MANDARINS.

Among Raw Celestials.

At the landing, four miles down a small stream from Nanking proper, Mr. L. and I had a novel experience while awaiting the arrival of the "up-steamer." To this landing, after our visit to the great Ming capital, we were kindly sent in the comfortable mission house-boat of the Presbyterian missionary, Mr. Lieman. We left at dark Wednesday evening, having arranged to sleep in the boat, near the landing, so as to be on hand on the arrival of the steamer next morning at 4 o'clock. As a matter of fact, the steamer did not come until the following morning at that hour, and there were about 200 Chinese to wait also during that thirty-six hours. That *was* a day! Not a word of our language did these Chinese understand, nor did we understand a dozen words of theirs. How they did swarm about us, and smile and chatter! How they did examine our clothing and all else about us, even Mr. L.'s false teeth, and quiz us! and how by degrees we succeeded, by mere good nature, by a few signs, and by Mr. L. letting them use his field-glass freely, in winning their favor and good will on every hand. Many of the characters interested us exceedingly. Tedious as the long waiting was, being required to keep our boatman, and sleeping two nights on the boat instead of one, yet we agreed that it was altogether providential; and it showed us a side of Chinese life of value to us, revealing Chinese character likewise in a truly practical way. I feel confident that under God I could win my way rapidly among these people, starting in without a word of the language or even a dictionary, and could persuade them, too, of the realities of the grace of God, as surely as I could the people of a raw community in America.

The truth is, it is the heart, and the spirit of God within it, mixed with tact and common sense, that wins anywhere. Those who cannot command those elements in America in a high degree should never come here. Mere sentiment or gush is not worth a rush here. Force of character that is not afraid also to come down and lose itself in the needs of the people, and be aflame, meanwhile, with a divinely begotten love, is the thing. You should have seen Miss Guinness to-day, while we were bargaining with a fellow in a crowded place at Kiu-Kiang, in less than two minutes' time getting hold of an audience of a few women and children, first by noticing a baby in its bright young mother's arms, gaining their confidence, and thus at once, a little aside from the crowd, enabled to introduce the gospel in a way that evidently impressed them.

A Gifted Missionary.

November 8.

It was a pleasure which I had scarcely anticipated, to have a meeting with Miss Guinness. The meeting occurred at Kiu-Kiang, where our steamer has been staying for a couple of hours, while the cargo was unloading. On the return we hope for another visit. As the steamer neared the landing-hulk, I saw over the heads of a host of Chinese people and several Catholic missionaries, twenty rods away, a tall lady, in blue cotton Chinese "maqua," and without bonnet, descending the stone steps from the water-front, or "Bund," as it is called, of the pretty shaded foreign concession, attended by a gentleman, also in Chinese costume. I at once took her to be the lady looked for.

A few minutes later, and our steamer was alongside the hulk, and the gentleman aforesaid approached the steamer's side, and said to me: "Is this Dr. Mabie? I am Mr. Eason of the C. I. M. Miss Guinness is waiting beyond the crowd to meet you." I was not long in skipping over the guards and elbowing through the swarming natives. I at once picked out the lady, who looked precisely as I had come to expect from her photograph and from the marked family resemblance especially to her dear father, whom she ardently loves, and concerning whom she could not speak without a tear glistening in the unusually joyful and soulful face. We went ashore, and took a stroll through the Bund and a street of curious Chinese shops, in search of a few trinkets, and then came back to the ship, and sat down for a "set-to" on all sorts of mission matters. She expressed delight at my going bodily into the mission enterprise. The expression of her own glowing interest and faith in the Christianization of the Chinese was inspiring enough.

She has just come through the country overland from Shanghai to Kiu-Kiang via Hangchow, Kinhwa, Takatang and the Poyang Lake, taking in a great stretch of canal and road travelling, and meeting China at home in a hundred forms, calling at and investigating station after station of Christian work.

She told of one work begun only a short time ago by a young Scotch girl from Glasgow, younger than herself, who had, in an incredibly short space of time, learned the language and gathered a church of 107 members. Miss Guinness saw eighty-four of them at the Lord's Supper. She emphasized the deep love the missionary had shown for the souls she had won, and assured me that her influence over them was unbounded. Miss Guinness feels beyond measure the importance of having a stamp of missionaries who can and will learn to deeply love the Chinese, and go right in, body and soul, among them, even eschewing foreign styles of houses and foreign ways of living. On this latter point, however, there are various opinions.

Well, it was refreshing to see and converse with the author of "In the Far East" and the daughter of my revered friend, Dr. Guinness. I shall also have double satisfaction in meeting the whole dear houshold when I reach London, since I shall have seen and known this gifted daughter and sister.

River Scenery.

The scenery of this mighty river, which for four successive days, in panoramic grandeur, we have been passing, is unique. Strangely, on one bank, the country is uniformly flat the whole distance. On the

LITTLE ORPHAN ISLAND.

other, the south bank, the scenery is greatly diversified, often majestic, with lofty peaks. The mountains, however, are for the most part bare, having long since been denuded of their forests. Occasionally, we see a stately island crowned with a monastery, or a quaint old town lying off a few miles distant on the slopes of hills, and walled in, over a distance of several miles square, with a picturesque wall, with frequent towers, which runs up the slopes, along the saddle-back of the range and down again to the water level of the river. Perhaps on a high, rocky promontory stands the citadel, with clusters of public buildings, including a temple and a pagoda. There are 1,200 walled cities in China, besides many of these walled towns.

We have on board the very intelligent British consul of Hankow, with his wife and daughter, just returned from England. The consul is an encyclopædia on China, having been twenty-nine years in the country; and he fills us up daily with all sorts of information and incidents. We have two Roman Catholic missionaries and one Wesleyan. In the other end of the ship, we have Chinese by the hundreds.

Hankow and Griffith John.

I found Brother Warner waiting on the landing-hulk at Hankow upon the arrival of our steamer, looking hale and hearty in his Chinese cap and cue. He had been waiting for me four days, having come down from Sui-fu in eleven days. In passing up through those same gorges of the upper Yang-tse two seasons ago, it took them over two months. Brother Warner also brought me a note of hearty greeting from Dr. John to come at once to his chapel and mission-house, his Sunday service being in session. An inspiring scene awaited us.

MR. WARNER IN NATIVE COSTUME

CHAPTER VIII.

Can the Chinese be Christianized?

CAN the thing be done? Are there facts on record that warrant our confidence in the achievements of grace upon a people stolid, anti-foreign, superstitious and gross as the Chinese in their heathen state appear to be? Take the following facts which were brought to my notice on a single Sabbath afternoon and evening while visiting Dr. Griffith John at Hankow. Dr. John is one of the really great missionaries of China — great in brain, in scholarly acquisitions, in command of the best mandarin dialect, in knowledge of the Chinese character, and in comprehensiveness of view of the scope and likewise of the limitations of true foreign mission enterprise. He has been once elected to the chairmanship of the Congregational Union of Great Britain, but declined the honor. After thirty years of service in the most difficult mission-field of the world, he prefers to toil on in the mine, rather than to accept any degree of conspicuous rope-holding at home. Is he choosing vainly?

Yesterday at 3 P.M. we went to Dr. John's chapel, a room capable of seating some 400 people. We went through a drenching rain, expecting to see a small congregation. Entering, we found a throng. Possibly seventy more persons could have been seated. We were a little late, and the service had begun. The congregation were singing, "I need thee every hour." A native sat at the organ, rolling out the strains in the best of form, and leading the singing with a confidence and a calm strength of feeling that would have been worthy of Sankey. A native pastor of large frame stood up and read the Scriptures, with an expression and depth of tone that fastened the attention of all. Fully one half of the congregation held Bibles, and followed the reading closely. Dr. John offered prayer. Every person in the congregation, except one feeble old octogenarian, arose, faced about, and knelt down upon the mats which usually rest on the stone floor underneath the simple benches. It was impressive to see the uniform rows of men in their clean blue cotton garments, their long cues hanging down their backs, every face buried in the hands, motionless on their knees before the true God. Dr. John preaches on the text, "Be ye steadfast, unmovable, always abounding in the work of the Lord." We discover at once a richness, a depth, a clear-cut and virile strength in the language, in pleasing contrast with the sing-song, nasal, whining dialects we have elsewhere heard, and Dr. John uses it with a finished mastery.

An Aged Believer.

Here at my left, and partly facing me, sits an old man of seventy, large spectacles on his nose, considerable gray beard on his chin, shrivelled in features, but very intent on the sermon. That man, I am told, lives six miles out in the country. He always walks to and from the chapel services on Sundays, and he doesn't miss two services in a year. He earns his living by selling cloth on the streets. He walks from his home to his trading-place every morning; but busy as he is, and toiling as he does, he yet finds time to devote two hours of five days in every week to preaching the gospel on the streets or in some one of several chapels. Lately his daughter-in-law, who had lived under his roof, died, and her family relatives and friends at her death urged that, according to the usual heathen custom, great quantities of silvered paper should be burnt in offerings, and that other heathen ceremonies should be carried out in behalf of her spirit. The old man objected, refused utterly, and, even though a mob of heathen beset his house for twenty-four hours, clamoring for the ritual with the vehemence of hyenas, he stoutly resisted, saying: "You may cut my head from my body if you will, but you shall never perform those ceremonies under my roof so long as I live, for I am a Christian." He had his way, and the mob subsided.

A Young Mandarin.

Here at my right sits an unusually intelligent young man of thirty. His clothing, a rich white brocaded satin over-vest, is evidence that he is of higher standing than those about him. On inquiry I find he is a young mandarin belonging to the official class. He is employed at present as a draughtsman in the office of the viceroy of the province, living in the city of Wuchang, just across the river from Hankow. Six months ago this young man was in some way attracted into Dr. John's chapel, and heard a sermon from one of the ablest native preachers. He was impressed, and came again. He began to seek interviews with other Christians. He sought Dr. John, and talked with him, saying, "I believe you have the true religion, and I want it." He began reading the Bible; he began worship in his family. It attracted the attention of his neighbors, and for five months he has been known openly as a Christian, and comes regularly to church. When solicited to apply for baptism, he frankly replied: "I have been for a year mildly smoking opium. I am not yet sure how great the power of the appetite may be over me. I will wait six months and see, seeking help to overcome it wholly."

He became especially fond of the hymn book. One hymn, based on the one hundred and third Psalm, was his favorite. A friend of his was recommended to read that hymn. The reference in the hymn to the "renewal of one's youth like the eagle's" puzzled the heathen friend, and he sought its explanation from the mandarin believer. He told him that it did not mean that his gray hairs should again become black, but that it described the renewal of one's spirit, the new birth and the refreshment which grace is ever supplying; and he added: "We have that spirit of God in our chapel, and I have it in my heart." "Oh, that's it!" said the astonished inquirer, and now he, too, is reaching out after the blessing.

Yesterday, the six months being ended, the young mandarin came to Dr. John's before service, and applied for baptism. He brought with him a present for the missionary, which I saw. It was a handsome fan, on which was written, by the giver's own artist hand, the texts: "If any man will come after me, let him deny himself, and take up his cross and follow me," and "He that loseth his life the same shall find it," and also the entire hymn beginning, "Ashamed of Jesus? that dear friend." This was his confession of faith.

A Blind Christian Boy.

"Did you observe that blind boy, yet in his teens, who sat just before me while I was preaching?" said Dr. John to us. "That boy is not only a Christian, but he is full of the Bible, having a remarkable memory. He knows substantially the whole New Testament. He literally carries the whole hymn book in his mind; and were you to come into our hospital to-morrow, where that boy often comes to pray for and with our patients, and join in our preliminary gospel service, he would stand up and repeat for you my entire sermon of to-day." Dr. John told us of how he first found out this boy, whose father had been a Christian for some time before him. The boy came to see the missionary, and said he was a Christian, and wished to join the church. Said the missionary, "Have you learned to pray?" "Yes," replied the boy. "Well, then," said the missionary, "let me hear you pray with me." They knelt together, the missionary first praying, and then the boy. Rising from their knees, the boy said, "That's the way my father taught me to pray." Thus from parents to children the gospel is being communicated in China.

Nor are these exceptional cases. Dr. John tells me that there are about 1,000 members enrolled in the churches attached to the London Missionary Society which are clustered about the city of Hankow. There are little clusters of these members living away in some scores of towns and villages. There were representatives of seven or eight provinces in the church service yesterday. Hankow, with its two suburban cities of Wuchang and Hanyan, and situated just at the junction of the Han River with the Yang-tse, is the chief inland trading-mart of the empire, and the representatives of several provinces are always coming and going for purposes of barter. Many of these, on their visits to Hankow, have been reached with the gospel, and going home have repeated the story, and thus have brought others. Dr. John tells me that even in the province of Hunan, the proudest and most anti-foreign district in China, into which no foreign missionary may yet safely enter, they have a considerable number of faithful members. But for results like these, one of the strongest men in China has wrought for thirty-five years, ably seconded by a force of some half-dozen missionary assistants, including a thorough Christian hospital, superintended by just the right sort of a physician and surgeon, Dr. Gillison, skilful and consecrated to the core. My heart was much moved by the narratives given me by this gifted young doctor of the blessing attending this far-reaching form of secondary mission enterprise.

CHAPTER IX.

The Western China Mission.

The Country and Modes of Travel.

November 12.

IF you would see China in one of its leading representative features, you must ascend one of its rivers, its main artery, the Yang-tse-Kiang. The river, for 1,000 miles upward, as far as Ichang, is navigable for ships of the largest tonnage, and fairly swarms with native junks, engaged in every species of rude traffic. There are villages and settlements all along its muddy banks, poor beyond description. The houses are mainly built of mere fagots of reeds, which grow in the swamp-lands that abound, especially on the north side of the river. The country on the south side of the river is in perfect contrast to this, being diversified by mountains and scenes of lofty grandeur.

Several cities, of large size and importance, are seen between Shanghai and Ichang. These are Chin-kiang (at the crossing of the Grand Canal, connecting Pekin with the South), Nanking, Wuhoo, Kiu-Kiang, Wuchang and Hankow. Each of these cities has a unique character of its own. Our present destination is Hankow, situated 600 miles from Shanghai. This Hankow is to the lower Yang-tse what St. Louis is to the lower Mississippi. Heavy navigation stops here; although in the near future, when treaty arrangements will admit of it, the upper river as far as Sui-fu, the St. Paul of China, 1,600 miles from the sea, will be opened to steam navigation. Steamers of a special pattern will need to be built for the purpose, inasmuch as the passage is through vast gorges or cañons, and up rapids swift and dangerous.

The present method of navigating this part of the river is by Chinese junks of great strength, built to endure much thumping on the rocks; and these junks are drawn by bamboo ropes, manned by coolies, — sometimes fifty in a string, — who walk along the foot-paths, often cut in the sides of precipitous rocks, rising hundreds, even thousands, of feet above them. Besides, two men in the boat, with long sweeps of oars, manage to shoot the boat around the rocks or jutting points of the shore. The tediousness and difficulties of making this ascent are considerable, especially when, as in the months of June and October, the waters often rise sixty feet above the ordinary. The tediousness may be conceived if you will recall that it usually consumes a time nearly twice as long as to come from Minneapolis to Shanghai. One can come down to Shanghai in about three weeks.

A striking impression was made on us, since our arrival in China, of the far-away character of the place, by the fact that whereas in telegraphing to one of our missionaries at Sui-fu via Chungking, we received a reply after three days, yet in arranging to meet him at Hankow, on his

ENTRANCE TO THE LU KAN GORGE

descent of the river, nearly three weeks would intervene; and were I to go up to Sui-fu to visit the brethren, Messrs. Upcraft and Warner, it would consume not less than three months to go and return.

Sz-chuen and the Mission.

Nevertheless, let it be borne in mind that the great province of Sz-chuen, in which this new station of ours is located, is the largest, and in many respects the most important province in all

MR. UPCRAFT'S BOAT.

China. This province has not been subject to the awful devastations, both from flood and flames of war, which have again and again laid in ruins the lower country of China. The material resources are immense, such as silk, tea, rice, wheat, corn, millet, tobacco, fruits, salt, sugar, medicines and minerals. The people live in better condition generally than in lower China. They have better houses. They have higher ideas and models, artistically, of homes, tombs and temples. There is greater variety of industry. Moreover, they are more open to foreign ideas, and in some parts there is a manifest hunger for knowledge. It is the seat of empire for Western China, and has many elements of a really independent state in itself. As early as the third century of our era, it was such an empire, known as the Kingdom of Shuh. In extent it covers 200,000 square miles, one half of which is mountainous and sparsely peopled. The population, however, at the lowest estimate, is 35,000,000. These various parts of the province, moreover, are easily accessible through the numerous rivers which flow southerly, emptying into the Yang-tse. One of these rivers, the Min, above Chentu, the capital, divides into ten or more streams flowing through the myriad-peopled plain on which the capital stands, and then they reunite to the southward.

MR. UPCRAFT.

Missionwise, this province has long been considered as one presenting rare possibilities. Roman Catholic priests entered it as early as 1700. From recent data it appears that there are three diocesan bishops in the province, ninety-six foreign priests (mostly Frenchmen), eighty-six native priests, many nuns and nurses, both foreign and native, and many catechists. Each diocese has two seminaries, and the number of believers claimed is 88,445. Most of these, unquestionably, are baptized infants. Nevertheless, we are assured that much influence of its peculiar sort has been gained over mandarins, high officials, and especially over the judges of local tribunals and over wealthy families.

But Protestants have also shown themselves appreciative of this field for mission work. The British and Foreign Bible Society has sent several colporters since 1868. The London Missionary Society, the English Wesleyans, and the Methodist Episcopal Church of America have all sent strong representatives into the district, and have the beginnings of good, permanent work inaugurated. Notably the China Inland Mission now occupies permanently ten stations, with forty-seven workers. At all of these points they are erecting or adapting permanent buildings for dispensaries, chapels, schools, hospitals, and residences. We Baptists, therefore, in sending our two single men, pioneers of our cause, eighteen months ago, into this great and promising field, — remote, indeed, and attended with its peculiar difficulties, — are by no means undertaking an unheard-of enterprise. We are glad to hear of speedy reinforcements promised from our Mission Rooms. We should have sufficient to occupy the populous and commanding points of Chung-king, just about to be opened as a treaty port, and Chentu, the capital, 175 miles north from Sui-fu, up the Min River, within the next fourteen months.

Messrs. Upcraft and Warner.

Since the Minnesota young people, in co-operation with the Missionary Union, took up this enterprise, the deepest missionary interest has been awakened in them, several of whom hope to enter the field when prepared. A systematic study and advocacy of the field has been instituted, and through their agency $1,500 is being annually raised in support of the pioneer missionaries.

THE CITY OF SUI-FU, WESTERN CHINA.

We gratefully record that within a few months, seven believers, first-fruits of the movement, have been baptized in connection with the labors of Messrs. Upcraft and Warner, and the first Baptist Church of Suifu has been organized. May this "handful of corn in the tops of the mountains yet shake like Lebanon."

A letter from Mr. Upcraft, which came to hand just as I left Shanghai for this up-river trip to Hankow, says: "I grieve that being within 1,000 miles, I shall not be able to see you; but prayer shall circle the globe for you, and desires that only God may know."

Sitting on the deck of this noble English steamer to-day, on this Nile of China, with pagoda-crowned rocks and promontories on the south bank, often glowing with the autumn tints of the maple and the tallow tree, or purple with the sparse herbage, and with the thickly peopled flat lowland on our north bank, despite all the thrill of novelty and pleasure which the experience affords, I, too, grieve that I can only send my yearning, prayer-laden glance up the gorges and over the mountains to where the dear brother in isolation courageously toils on for Christ at Sui-fu. Like one of old, I am only permitted to scan the borders of the land, but may not enter. I have at least knelt in prayer at the hither base of the great mountain range which separates us in person, while by faith we have met. It is at least a satisfaction, beyond all power of words to express, to have traversed even thus far the course over which these past and future pilgrims for Central Asia's evangelization have devoutly come, and will come until He whose right it is shall reign universally and supreme.

CHAPTER X.

The Southern China Mission.

Hongkong.

November 18.

WE are entering Hongkong Harbor. The high hills are on every side, in a vast mountainous amphitheatre. Stately chalk-white European buildings rise on all the slopes, some of them alabastrian in beauty. The smoke of numerous shops and manufactories shadows some of the slopes, but for the most part there is a sort of a New Jerusalem-like whiteness and beauty about the whole place. Would it were so morally!

Hongkong is an English colony. What there is of Chinatown is obscured or by no means prominent. A noble English cathedral rests on one shoulder of the mountain; and on the very summits, reached by cable railways, are great hotels, villas and country seats, baronial in splendor and spaciousness. European merchants and army and customs officials do not come out here to live in huts or in native fashion.

Great steamships are running in and out of the harbor as we enter. Twenty-seven of them are in sight, several of them going to Japan, some to Australia, some arriving from Singapore, England, etc. This is the *third largest port of transit in the world!* First London, then Liverpool, then Hongkong. We now approach the landing, and sampans swarm around, eager to take us ashore.

Arrival at Swatow.

November 20.

The sail from Hongkong to Swatow was of only a day and a night. The seas, however, ran high, and our tub of a steamer danced about like a cork, and we found the distance quite sufficient for our gastric powers.

HONGKONG HARBOR.

The city of Swatow itself has few attractions. It lies on a low, flat point of ground, but it is evidently a port of considerable commercial importance. A very rich agricultural country, inside a mountain range, lies north and west of it. On this great fertile Tie Chiu district, I should think never afflicted with famine, our mission lies. The English Presbyterians share the field with us. They have extensive compounds adjacent to the city proper; and by means of schools, a great hospital and a very aggressive evangelism also, they are pressing things vigorously. We have a mission chapel in the city, but our compound lies across the bay a mile or two distant, on high, rocky terraces, most picturesquely situated. For beauty it exceeds any mission we have seen in Japan or China. For this, thanks to the diligence, painstaking care and taste of Dr. Ashmore. When he purchased the tract many years ago for the Missionary Union, at the nominal sum of $500, it was little more than a pile of verdureless, decomposing granite, and as unattractive as possible. But by dint of continuous planting of trees and shrubs, by cutting the way for paths and terrace plats for buildings of half a dozen sorts, this Judean-like wilderness has been transformed into a very garden of the Lord, fit emblem of the spiritual transformations also being carried on under the leadership of a gardener skilled in moral, as in natural, culture. It was our privilege to see many of these " trees of righteousness, the planting of the Lord's hand," coming on to maturity and beauty in and about that enclosure.

DR. ASHMORE'S HOUSE.

We have here four good houses for missionary families, besides a hospital, boys' and girls' schools, a training-school for preachers, and a chapel. There is much to gladden one. Then better than all, there are thirty stations out in the great plains back from Swatow, up the rivers and canals, some of which we are to visit. More than 1,100 members have been enrolled.

Brother Foster and Dr. Ashmore met us at the little landing on the compound as our sampan from the steamer touched, and we were shown up the hill to the mission-house, where a dozen or so of our workers soon met us. Brethren Campbell and Norvell had come in from the Hakka district to see us. The Scotts and Carlins are also tabernacled here. Misses Scott, Campbell and Dunwiddie, who left America since I did, we found here two weeks ahead of us.

We made an interesting round of the compound to the various schools,— the evangelists' training-school, the Bible-women's school, the hospital and chapel. At all these places we were met with hearty and polite greetings from the native Christians, all indicating that they had been anticipating our arrival. On later occasions we were called out for addresses to them, and their responses were tender and touching. The following is a sample, spoken to us before Dr. Ashmore's sermon on Sunday morning by the pastor, Po-san:—

"We thank you for coming so far to see us. Forty years ago, no such sight as you now see,

SWATOW PREACHERS AND STUDENTS.

in this full house of men, women and children, worshipping the true God, was possible. The people then had no Bible; they were devil worshippers; they despised women and children. We thank the Christians in America for sending us the missionaries of forty years ago and since, to give us the Bible and all attendant blessings. As you journey on in your course from land to land, please to bespeak for us the prayers of Christians in all countries."

While this was spoken, the men rose and stood. Afterwards one of the Bible-women made a similar address of welcome, all the women saying their "Amen."

Inland on the Swatow Field.   November 25.

Much to our satisfaction, an expedition was planned for us into the country, mid dense heathenism itself. On Monday morning the two mission-boats were gotten ready, stocked with provisions and conveniences, and adequately manned. The mission-boat is an institution worth noting. Often for weeks together it must serve the missionary, and sometimes his family, for transportation, inn, retreat, and defense from the inquisitive gaze and obtrusiveness of the curious and often rude multitudes. Without it, it is difficult to see how in China the most real mission work in the country could be done at all.

SWATOW BIBLE-WOMEN.

One living in America can have no idea of how numerous, on the great plains of China, are the rivers and canals. They often run in a vast network through and through thousands of square miles of level country. They are the main thoroughfares. All the cities and towns of consequence are built upon them. There are rarely any other public roads, as we count roads.

This mission-boat, therefore, is a *sine qua non* in a missionary's equipment. A good one costs about $300 (no more than a good carriage at home). It is about thirty-five feet in length, and ten in width. In the centre is a house room, about eight by twelve feet in size, with room for two narrow beds at the sides, a table at the end, and shelves for a few books. A pantry and a closet adjoin at one end, while outside and in a sort of forecastle the boatmen and assistant evangelists live and sleep. The cooking is done on deck. The boat has a mast, and may be propelled either by a sail or by long oars worked by coolies. On our expedition we had two of these boats, one of them formerly used by Miss Field in her extensive tours among the Tie Chiu women.

We had with us, besides Dr. Ashmore and Brother Foster, four evangelists, a cook and six boatmen. For the first half-day, taking advantage of the tide, we floated lazily up the wide stream which issues into the Swatow Bay.

At length, about sunset, a town is reached at a junction of two streams. Just before we anchor, to prepare for an evangelizing service on the banks, a boat approaches us from one of the streams, having on board several men and boys. Two of the men are dressed in clean, new buff suits of cotton clothing. Their faces beam with intelligence and interest. Our two missionboats are old acquaintances of theirs. They readily divine what missionaries are in them. By the peculiar telegraphy begotten of Christian fellowship, the news has someway reached them that the two American visitors are likewise coming, and so these two dear evangelists have come out as did the ancient brethren to Appii Forum and the Three Taverns, to Paul, to greet us.

We all anchor, and they come on board, and most politely and formally present to us their salutations. These two men have been out for six weeks in a round of evangelizing. One of them brings a simple map of the district they have traversed, with their route traced in red ink. They have gone "two and two," apostle-like. They have enjoyed it much, have found respectful hearing, have sold many Scriptures and tracts. "Wouldn't they like to give it up, and return to idolatry?" I ventured to ask one of them. The reply came with electric vehemence, "No! it would fill my heart with misery." When this man was converted, his mother was a wizard; she used to climb knife-ladders and walk on live coals of fire, and practice many enchantments. When the son told her of his decision, she replied, "You are right, and I will join you." "That woman," said the son, "now has forty-two descendants who have ceased from idol worship."

While we were thus conversing, Dr. Ashmore and an evangelist have begun preaching to the villagers who swarm about them on shore. A few minutes later, and my man is also at it with boldness and fervor. Paul's argument at Lystra or on Mars Hill, or some other apostolic precedent, is by these men, Ashmore-trained, as a rule followed everywhere; and some with the same kinds of effect. Some believe; others look sceptical, and many scoff. Frequently one comes again, or asks a question revealing anxiety to know the truth. The universal testimony is, "The doctrine is good, but hard to put in practice." Some have heard before; all confess to guilt.

DR. ASHMORE.

Evening.— Again we anchor alongside a fleet of General Ah-Pung's gunboats. Dr. Ashmore is calling to me to come on, that we may hold a little meeting in the village. I act as the stool pigeon while Dr. Ashmore draws the gospel net. We sally out, Dr. Ashmore and his two students in training as evangelists, and cross the rice-fields for a half-mile, ferrying a canal by a boat, managed by a leper.

We approach a town snugly ensconced under a lot of grand spreading banyan trees, which would appear to be one or two hundred years old. We thread our way through a narrow street, followed by a crowd of inquisitives, inexpressibly filthy and vile in person and speech, and enter an open space. There taking our stand, Dr. Ashmore starts off one evangelist, and at a little distance another. A hundred people have surrounded us. First and nearest in the inner circle is a lot of small boys; then larger boys; then those taller still; then stalwart men; and hovering on the outside of the circle a number of women. To stand in the centre of a crowd like that, having every eye gazing into yours as if to bore you through with inquiry, to think that it is the only time you will ever thus face that crowd, and they destitute of hope for this life or the next, and be unable to speak — ah, my brother in America! complacent over the state of the heathen while you luxuriate in all Christian privileges, put yourself there, and you'll not be indifferent.

I accepted the bench a man brought me, and in a moment more the youthful native evangelist began. At once he reminds them of the true God who reigns above, who gives the rains and

BANYAN TREE.

fruitful seasons from heaven, etc. A moment more, and a little bullet-eyed man, the least intelligent-looking one of the crowd, breaks out: "You say there is a heaven. Of course there is a heaven and a God in it; else how should we get anything to eat?" The heathen are not the ignorant creatures we take them to be. The first sermon was about three minutes long.

Then Dr. Ashmore began, and for five minutes more he gave them an apostolic broadside. Eloquent always, he is peculiarly himself with a heathen audience before him. As he made point after point on God, sin, judgment, pardon through Christ, heaven and hell, there was riveted attention. It was a study to watch their faces. Several kept nodding assent, as point after point was made. It was perfectly evident that they recognized as true the great salient points made.

It was also, alas! just as evident that most of them took it just as sinners do at home. They said: "It is true, but the trouble is in my business, as opium-selling or idol-making. I can't afford to submit to the truth."
"When they knew God, they glorified him not as God."
As we departed, said the doctor to me: "A few years ago in a village like this, we would have been hooted out of town under showers of gravel stones; but now, note the respectful attention."
Coming back to the boat, many followed us. All were respectful; and as we came along the bank to our boat, passing three or four rude gunboats of General Ah-Pung lying near, one of the soldiers asked Dr. Ashmore, "Venerable teacher, have you had your rice?" That is better than the epithet "foreign devil," with which in the past the missionaries used to be saluted. Still, you

OUR CARRIAGE.

must not imagine that there is much in such a locality as this but the rankest heathenism, squalor, ignorance, poverty and misery. Heathenism is something *awful*, especially in China.

There is light in the gloom, however. While I am writing (it is 8 o'clock in the evening), out on the deck of our boat, our good cook, a deacon of the Swatow church, is holding forth in the moonlight to a few natives about him, preaching the gospel to them with the intensest feeling. Brother Foster tells me he is expatiating on "The Character of the True, the Highest, the Holiest God." "Our work is to call men to the way of righteousness, the way of peace, the way of heaven. This way is narrow. The way of the opium-eater is broad, so men don't like this," etc. Now he is straightening out the Fung Shway superstition in good style. Now he is urging the blessedness of the Sabbath. Now he gives a parable. The essentials of the way of salvation are now being urged. Now the verse of a hymn rises on the evening air. And so the dear good man goes on. He has just added: "The merits of Christ are beyond compare. It's no use to worship your ancestors," etc. May the Spirit send the truth home to his little audience! All day long the man has kept this up.

Chao-chow-fu.

November 26.

This morning we rose at 5 o'clock, and leaving our house-boats to be returned to Swatow, we prepared to strike across the country about six miles to Chao-chow-fu, the next largest city to

Canton in this province of Kwan-tung. We had four sedan chairs, each borne on the shoulders of two strong coolies, and several porters for the baggage. Besides these were our preachers and cook. This does not reckon in the escort of small boys, Chinese dogs, and occasionally a *black pig* or two, which from village to village volunteered their escort.

Our route was along a serpentine, narrow roadway or path ; the usual style of passageway in China running directly through the fields, there never being such a thing anywhere as a fence or a piece of land laid out at right angles. These roads are often made of concrete, smooth and well finished. All along as we came, there were patches of sugar cane, rice-fields, turnips and

CHINESE TOMBS.

cabbages. All sorts of small farming is here carried to a high pitch of economic cultivation. Every particle of sewage, such as in America is commonly wasted, is preserved in great earthen jars, and used upon the fields. The smells, to say the least, rival those of Cologne. Villages are huddled in at intervals of every half-mile or so, and the emblems of idolatry and ancestral worship are everywhere seen.

Having arrived at the city of Chao-chow-fu, we found it like all others that I have seen in its general features — its buildings of stone or cement crowded closely together, in which the people herd like swine, with narrow streets indescribably filthy. Of course the entrance into the town of four foreigners was the signal for a sensation of the first order. Barnum's Circus was never eyed more intensely than was our procession: for the four hours we were in the city, we were amid a lot of hangers-on.

We visited our little native chapel, where we met a couple of evangelists. We called at the Presbyterian Hospital, and found 100 patients in waiting. Here we saw a poor victim of opium under treatment, *chained to his bed*. He had been there twice before, but each time had run away to indulge his raging appetite, so fearfully did he suffer. The third time he came of his own accord, and begged to be chained, that he might be compelled to remain the fifteen days necessary for treatment. His distressed father, a Christian preacher, sat by his bedside trying to comfort and encourage his poor boy. As we knelt to pray with the sorrowing yet courageous couple, never did I realize more vividly the awful curse that the opium traffic has thrust upon poor benighted China.

We next visited a Confucian Temple, the Examination Halls, and especially Gold Hill, a high lookout on one side of the city, from which a superb view was had. From this hill we could take in a wide range of city, country, river, and especially mountain scenery.

The most impressive feature was the vast area of mountain-sides, on the northwest side of the city, completely covered, from the lofty summits away down into the valley and plains, with graves. In this case the graves are marked with gray stones at the head of the small mounds. It seemed to me there was an extent of several hundred acres completely filled; and Dr. Ashmore tells me that in many cases the graves are filled *three deep!* For ages and ages the dead have been carried there. It was to us melancholy in the extreme, radiant as was the sunshine that gilded the purpled hills. It was like a look into some illuminated Gehenna, symbolic of China's whole civilization—an ancient sepulchre, but a sepulchre still. But resurrection life has begun to stir in this valley of dry bones, and these bones shall yet live and stand upon their feet, an exceeding great army. May the Lord hasten it in His time!

A Quaint Bridge.

At Chao-chow-fu there is a quaint old bridge over the river, probably 1,500 feet in length, a curious combination of stone arch, wood and pontoon. About a third of the way across the stream, the stone-work ceases; and descending some massive stone steps, you come upon the pontoon part, which crosses the main channel of the river. This pontoon can be opened to admit the passage of tall-masted boats. Passing this section, you ascend to the main bridge again. There are some fifteen or sixteen large stone piers in the bridge, between which stretch long stone slabs, about forty feet in length, which form the bridge floors. But what is especially remarkable, on each of these piers are clustered several buildings—shops, in which all sorts of trade are carried on. The buildings extend balcony-like over the outer edges of the piers, and are "shored" up by poles which extend down into the river-bed, to help support the buildings. To cap all, in several cases, a large banyan tree is growing directly out of the side of a pier, covering the huddle of shops with its grateful shade. These Chinese are original. For a bridge, this is the most unique thing I have seen.

The Hakkas.

At Chao-chow-fu we saw many specimens of the Hakka people and of their numerous boats, anchored below the quaint old bridge which spans the river which issues from the Hakka country. It was no small disappointment to Brother Campbell that we were unable to go out into the Hakka district, where he has been pioneering for two or three years. Brother Campbell describes these people as being a distinct race among the various branches of the Chinese people. They claim to have originally come from the Fo-Kien Province, about 600 years ago. Dr. Eitel says respecting them: "If the Maotze or mountain tribes of West China may be described as the Britons, the Cantonese as the Saxons, and the Haklos as the Danes of Chinese civilization, the Hakkas must be characterized as the Normans."

MR. CAMPBELL.

They are superior to other Chinese people in fondness for education, in refusing the foot-binding of their women, and in other important respects. Their dialect is the connecting link between the Cantonese and the Mandarin, resembling closely the latter. They occupy parts of five provinces. If we ever mean to permanently strike the roots of our work inland from the old and well-worked station of Swatow, it seems as if the work among the Hakkas should be reinforced and pressed. With this Dr. Ashmore strongly agrees. Brethren Campbell and Norvell have explored the district widely in several directions, and report the people as friendly, willing to purchase tracts and Scriptures, and tolerant of foreigners desiring to live in the region. The Lutherans have an extensive work among them, and the English Presbyterians are effecting entrance also.

Last Sabbath I had a most delightful interview with Brother Campbell's Hakka teacher, who has lately been converted. He is an unusually handsome fellow, of fine features, light complexion and graceful figure. His hands impressed me as exceedingly graceful, with long, tapering fingers and the whitest of nails. He was clad in a long, clean sky-blue tunic, white stockings and satin shoes. His answers to my searching questions were touching. Brother Campbell interpreted. We prayed together. On departing, the dear fellow wished Mr. Campbell to say to me that he "was ten times glad to have seen me, and that he thought I was ten times good to take so much interest to come and see Chinaman, and talk kindly with him."

There is special satisfaction to me in these face-to-face talks with such trophies of grace met with in these lands. I do not find it difficult to love the Chinese. The image of Christ in them, either real or prospective, fascinates one beyond measure.

This afternoon we are all aboard a Hakka boat which we engaged at Chao-chow-fu, and are having a delightful sail down the Han River. We are floating past banyan and banana groves,

A HAKKA BOAT.

by orange orchards loaded with the tempting golden fruit, along sand bars yellow in the sunshine, past pagodas old and shrub-grown, — all in decay, — meeting and passing all sorts of odd and primitive river crafts. To-morrow will be your Thanksgiving Day.

November 27.

We are just leaving for Hongkong again. Brother Foster came off with us to the steamer, Dr. Ashmore bidding us farewell from the pier, and tenderly turning back to his continued work. The dear old servant of Dr. Ashmore, Deacon Siau Thong, whose preaching on the boat I have mentioned, also came with us to the steamer. What a grip he gave us, and such a smile, and petition to pray for him, as he laid down our luggage on the deck and turned to descend the ladder. Now we are off. Again the little mission-boat turns back to the self-imposed exile for Jesus' sake. We move out through the straits into the broad sea, which laves all shores, and from its very vastness proclaims the unity of all lands and all human kind. The several white houses of the mission compound yonder, peering through the foliage and rising on the bold rocks, stand firm and glowing in the evening sunset. From the wide veranda of the house standing on the highest peak, Dr. Ashmore's house, we faintly see (for it is a mile away) a group of shadowy figures, and can just discern a waving handkerchief. It seems to say to us again: "Don't forget us in the home-land! pray for us, and send us helpers." We return the salute. The heart sighs its sympathy and fellowship, and audibly we say, "God bless, keep and reward them!" We turn also a glance across to the other shore, to take in the row of a half-dozen houses of the Presbyterian Mission, and breathe a similar prayer. A few minutes later, as we rapidly move away, the shores vanish from our sight, while in memory, sympathetic and blessed, the scene remains indelible forever.

DEACON SIAU THONG.

CHAPTER XI.

Canton and Macao.

November 29.

AGAIN we are aboard a great river boat, as large and fine as anything on the Hudson, and we are steaming up the river ninety miles to Canton. The glow of the tropical twilight reddens the whole western sky, and tints the far-spreading bay, and makes the mountains roseate, so that again we float as in a dreamland of beauty. A half-dozen passengers in the cabin and some hundreds of Chinese in the second cabin and steerage, fill the ship, and remind us where we are.

A comfortable night is passed, and at 7 o'clock we arrive at the steamer's wharf in Canton, amid a sea of floating Chinese houses, including even floating hotels; a peculiarity of Canton being that not less than 200,000 people live in boats on the river. These are the only homes these people ever know. There are 800,000 living in the city; but these live, rear their families, and ply their trades wholly in boats, — house-boats of all sizes and descriptions. Many of them are rowed by women and girls, often by a mother with a baby tied to her back. The woman stands up in the stern of the boat, and sculls with a long sweep, swaying to and fro — a motion which the baby seems to enjoy, often falling asleep under it. It is common to see a two-year-old child at the end of a cord by which it is tied for safety, straining over the edge of the boat to look into the water, or to watch the movements in the boat next door to it. As our steamer landed, Brother Simmons met us, and took us to the mission-house of our Southern Convention Board. Here we met Dr. R. H. Graves and wife and a pleasant circle of missionary sisters.

Dr. Graves and Mr. Simmons are both veterans on the field, and thoroughly at home among the Chinese. Over 600 members have been gathered into the churches, planted in seven or eight stations. During the last year some seventy-five additions were won from among the heathen. Dr. Graves' method of training his converts and gathering from among them the more promising as evangelists and pastors, struck us as admirable. All new-made converts, as a rule, are brought in at intervals for several weeks of each year, and pass through a sort of testing process under Dr. Graves' hand. It is not strange that many a young David, one anointed of God, thus sought, is found among the sons of Jesse. The women's work is here also well handled under the skilled direction of Misses Whilden, Hartwell, McMinn and others. A fine lot of girls are being trained for all good things.

Canton, Sunday, November 30.

This morning we went to the native church here, a body of some 300 members. It was a refreshing sight to see the native pastor preaching with such earnestness and power. (Text 1 Thess. ii. 13.) A church meeting followed. A woman was received and baptized. This church is self-supporting wholly; in fact, supports two churches besides. The work of our Southern brethren here is flourishing. There are only three male missionaries.

I have just been to their afternoon Sunday school, and given them a fifteen-minute talk, which Dr. Graves interpreted. Their eyes kindled as if it struck in. I am getting to like this speaking through an interpreter. I find the pauses between paragraphs give me time to pack in the tersest

FLOATING HOUSES.

things, and they some way go home. In a service of Mr. Herring's at Shanghai, I had spoken with considerable liberty on the power which Christ imparts to us when we welcome himself, and not a mere doctrine about him, into our hearts, and illustrated it pretty freely. Mr. Herring interpreted freely for me, and the eyes of my hearers were sparkling; but when Mr. Herring had finished, a coolie member of the church, in the back part of the room, not satisfied with the interpretation, arose, and, turning to his companion coolies, several of whom were about him, went all over the matter again, reinterpreting Mr. Herring's interpretation, and finally wound up

SCENE NEAR MACAO.

by saying: "That's what he said, and it has warmed my heart and done me good, and I want it to do you good." This man was a member of the church, but for years has not been heard before to say a word in any of the meetings. He was a poor fellow, bare-footed, who earns his living by water-carrying at 7 cents a day. Thus one backslider was unearthed. It effected quite a sensation in the church.

Yesterday we went to tiffin at the American consul's, by invitation. Hon. Charles Seymour of La Crosse, Wis., is the capable incumbent. He and his accomplished wife, who had heard me preach to the people of the foreign settlement the night before, gave us cordial welcome and genuine hospitality. Dr. Happer of the Presbyterian Mission, a veteran in China, and Mr. Simmons were also invited. We were most agreeably entertained, and the consul gave us much light respecting treaty relations between our government and China. He has had good success in securing indemnities from the Chinese government in cases where mission properties have from time to time been destroyed by mobs.

The Tomb of Morrison.

MACAO HARBOR, 6 P.M.

Well, we have put in a few hours in doing this quaint old Portuguese town (colonized by the Portuguese over 300 years ago), and are off by another steamer for Hongkong to-night. We here found the L.'s, just out from Minneapolis. Mrs. L. was in our late institute a pupil of mine. How little I anticipated such a meeting in China, on the day when this sister first called on me, desiring to enter my training class, to better prepare for her intended work. This is the third of my own pupils I am meeting on the mission-fields — one in Japan, one in China, and I trust one in Assam.

They were delighted to see us, and they went with us to visit Morrison's grave, and the garden in memoriam of Camoëns, the poet, who here wrote the "Lusiad." We also called on the McCloys, missionaries of the Southern Board. Dr. Morrison, his wife Mary, and his son J. R. all sleep in plain stone sarcophagi in one corner of a very prettily kept cemetery. It was an impressive thing to stand there for a few moments. What Carey was to India, Morrison was to China. It is eighty-two years since he landed in China. He translated the Scriptures and compiled a Chinese dictionary, and for twenty-seven years pioneered everything good for China. He won perhaps a dozen converts, yet in the main he died without the sight for which his lofty spirit yearned. We trod reverently the ground about that tomb in the southeast corner of the walled cemetery. We plucked a leaf from the tree which droops over the square stone sarcophagus which contains the dust of one of the greatest of earth's victors, and breathed a deeper prayer for China's millions.

The city is very picturesquely situated on hills, and many are the buildings which present a striking semi-European appearance. There is a fine old ruin of a cathedral long since burned. The place is largely Catholic, of course, there being some 7,000 Portuguese living here. The blight on the place, however, is in the fact that it is the great gambling-place of the whole region, — the Baden-Baden of China, — people coming to it from Hongkong and elsewhere, both men and women, Europeans as well as natives, and spending Sundays gambling with desperation.

CHAPTER XII.

Medical Mission Work in China.

The Claim Made for It.

IS this a properly distinctive undertaking for Christian missions to engage in? Should we so highly regard the body and the treatment of its maladies? Can a mission force afford to become a hospital staff? Will it not be so cumbered and harassed by unfortunates of every description as to practically preclude the exercise of the higher spiritual functions? Is it not a confession of failure for Christianity to turn from humanity in its virility and vigor, and address itself so prominently to the invalided? Should we not aim to meet the heathen in their strength, and conquer them on the high places of the field?

Since coming to China, queries like these have forced themselves upon us. It is claimed by some that the real nature of Christianity renders works of mercy like these of fundamental importance for their own sake; and, again, that it is an arrangement in the economy of grace that those who will attend to these primal wants and woes of men in Christ-like fashion, are sure to be honored by the Saviour of men in finding the way thus opened for a speedier and surer reception of the gospel. It must be confessed that our Lord thus wrought in His earthly ministry. He desired mercy rather than sacrifice, and He always won sacrifice to His service in quarters where conviction was produced of the reality and depth of His mercy.

When that chief of prophets, John the Baptist, amid his dire sorrows and persecutions, fell into a momentary fit of doubt, and sent to Jesus for reassurance of faith, Jesus replied: "Go your way, and tell John what things ye have seen and heard; how that the blind see, the lame walk, the lepers are cleansed, the deaf hear, the dead are raised, to the poor the gospel is preached."

NESTORIAN TABLET.

Jesus indeed wrought these merciful signs by miracle; but Christianity in the world is a standing miracle, and the healing art of modern science is one of the miracles of Christianity.

The evangelical results already achieved in some successful missions have been reached through a large regard to the physical woes as well as to the spiritual needs of the people. These means have proved availing to awaken appreciation of the temper of missions, and to enable the natives to discriminate between their real friends and their enemies among foreigners. Merciful healing ministries may then be regarded, and, in fact, are regarded, not of the nature of a lure, but of an authentication of something unselfish and divine.

A prominent missionary put the whole thing in a nutshell when he said to us: "Hospital ministrations are a safe form of showing kindness to the Chinaman." The Chinaman in his native state is nothing if not avaricious. The novice, therefore, on coming as a missionary to China, needs to be put on his guard from the moment he reaches San Francisco to take the steamer, that any intended kindness to John in the way of moneyed gratuity is misdirected, and sure to awaken his self-interest rather than gratitude. Yet certainly he who would benefit people with the gospel must first establish a friendly relation, and especially among the heathen, where many well-warranted and deep-seated suspicions against foreigners have been planted. In the view of many who have tried it, the Christian hospital is one of the least objectionable methods that can be employed in China.

How It Works.

When a man has become an in-patient in a hospital (not a mere hanger-on of a dispensary), where probably he must lie in bed for several days or weeks, and while under treatment must observe unselfish, unpaid-for skilful attention from the Christian surgeon or nurse, he will begin to study about it. It is then his heart will melt and open. For the first time since he was born, he will realize what benevolence is. This sense is fundamental to any apprehension of the gospel. It is also index of a radical change in the man's estimate of the missionary as a representative of the gospel. The Christ-like has dawned on the heathen. Still further, when the patient shall have recovered and returned to his home, he will carry the report and spirit of the place where he has found healing. Again, as in Christ's time, the mercy shown becomes the authentication of a heavenly mission. Dr. Gillison of Hankow told us that he had often been thrilled with delight to observe the awakening of appreciation, and so of a man's moral sense, as if by miracle, as the result of some slight attention bestowed on a patient. It might be from only the tucking in of a man's foot exposed to a draught of air. He further testified that as the result of two operations for cataract on the eyes of two sisters from one household, a village was opened to the gospel, nearly a whole clan was converted, and a promising church organized.

Connected with all the hospitals are gospel halls, in which services are daily held, which patients in waiting must attend before they have access to the consulting-rooms. Evangelists and Bible-women here render service in the wards for men and women respectively. On all the walls are hung handsome and striking texts of Scripture to greet the eye, and burn their way into the memories of the sufferers, who observe them for weeks together.

The Present Status.

There are at present sixty-one hospitals and forty-four additional dispensaries in connection with our Protestant missions in China, and last year there were 350,000 patients. Of course none would claim that evangelical impressions were made upon so large a number. We have taken pains personally to inspect six of these institutions, located respectively at Shanghai, Nan-

HOSPITAL AT SWATOW.

king, Hankow, Ningpo, Swatow, and Canton, and looked up the workings of as many more. We gleaned the following facts: —

In the Margaret Williamson Hospital for women at Shanghai, there were 9,000 patients the first year it opened, and 27,000 prescriptions filled. At our own hospital at Ningpo, now in charge of Dr. Grant, founded by the untiring devotion of Dr. Barchet, who wore himself out in this service, it was a common thing to have 300 patients daily, and 10,000 in a single year. In the Presbyterian hospital at Swatow last year, in which there were 5,830 persons treated and 1,129 operations performed, the patients came from 1,780 towns and villages through four prefectures.

For fifty-six years the hospital in Canton has been pouring forth a stream of practical benevolence, the reflex benefit of which has been reaped by all denominations. Its Chinese name, translated, is "The Hospital of Broad and Free Beneficence," and the locality about it is known as "The Great Street of Benevolence and Rectitude." It was my privilege twice to preach there to English-speaking people. The present senior surgeon, Dr. J. G. Kerr, has been in service thirty-five years, in which time there have been over half a million patients and 25,000 operations.

Besides all this, Dr. Kerr has found time to really lay the foundations of a medical college. For years he has had in training certain promising assistants, some thirty of whom have taken a full and systematic course and obtained certificates. One of these we saw lecturing to a class on anatomy, manipulating a manikin. Another, Dr. Soto-meng, stands unrivalled in operations for cataract. Another is a specialist in eutropium. Nor is this all. Dr. Kerr has prepared and published in Chinese a series of text books, embracing the subjects of physiology, hygiene, diagnosis, chemistry, materia medica and surgery, thus providing a basis for the development of medical science in the empire.

The expense is relatively small. The necessary buildings are not costly. In most cases even these are the gifts of individual philanthropists. For example, the fine large establishment of the Methodists, which I visited at Nanking, to my pleasant surprise, I found was the gift of former acquaintances at Oak Park, Ill. This is known as "The Philander Smith Memorial Hospital." The family have established similar institutions in Japan, India and the United States. Could this family see what my eyes saw in and about that place in Nanking, — the thronged chapel, with out-patients in waiting ; the earnest evangelist dispensing the Word ; the bright assistants and nurses, trophies of the work, now serving in the dispensary and wards, — and could they see the proofs I saw of the commanding influence which the beloved Dr. Robert Beebe, in charge, has gained over the city as a whole, they would rejoice deeply in their investment. We saw a dozen costly banners, the gifts of mandarins and wealthy Chinese citizens, which had been presented in token of their appreciation of so beneficent an institution. Similar tokens are to be seen in all Chinese hospitals. Several viceroys, including his excellency Li Hung Chang and his lady, are regular contributors to these institutions of mercy and good will.

Patients usually provide their own beds and food ; the services of physicians, nurses and medicines being furnished gratuitously. At the most, the mission boards pay only the salary of

LI HUNG CHANG.

the medical missionary. The foreign residents in all the cities are accustomed to subscribe from $1,000 to $2,000 annually towards the expenses. They pay fees besides for personal services, as do the wealthy Chinese; and, moreover, the Chinese people often subscribe to the support of the hospital, as in Swatow last year, about $400 was given.

Results.

In many cases the soul-saving results are disappointing. In several hospitals, however, we heard mention of say twenty additions a year to the churches. It is a principle usually to receive none for baptism at the hospital itself. Patients are required first to go away to their homes, and prove, by a probation of consistent living, their real change. The testimony of missionaries is general, however, that in extended country tours of visitation of out-stations, it is a common thing to receive application for baptism from former hospital patients, or those influenced by them.

Said Dr. John to the writer: "So highly do I value the mission hospital that, assuming that you have a thoroughly trained and truly consecrated man in charge of it, if I could have my way, I would have a hospital at every central station opened in China." From the beginning he has had a good hospital. His estimate may be too sanguine.

The writer is concerned to know if some friend of the Missionary Union will not volunteer to put in a plant, costing say $10,000, at Sui-fu, Western China, our new station, where Upcraft and Warner are so heroically breaking ground. Such a provision would place Dr. Finch in a position, in a new district, to test the value of medical work as authenticating the gospel.

CHAPTER XIII.

Equatorial Asia.

French China.

SAIGON, COCHIN CHINA, December 7.

THIS is an important city of the French Colony in Cambodia. All steamers of the French line from Japan and China to Marseilles stop here for cargo and passengers. We arrived this morning, and are spending the day here; not at all because it is Sunday, for evidently no such thing as a Christian Sunday is much recognized in these parts, even if sea-going vessels were able or disposed to observe the day.

This place is not quite on the sea-coast, but up the Mekong River, perhaps thirty miles from the coast. The city, as to its buildings, has quite a European air, though very unlike the more English cities of Shanghai or Hongkong. The red tile roofs and the yellow stucco, which one sees so much in France, prevail here. The population is most mongrel. There are the French army and Custom House officials in white duck suits and white pith helmet hats; there are numerous Chinese; then there are the native Assamese, with occasional Siamese and Malays. Many wear the turban and a gay sort of skirt, with sometimes a bright brocaded wrap about the shoulders. The French officials and merchants use many of the blacker fellows for coachmen and servants generally.

All day long they have been lolling about the shaded Bund along the steamer landing, or driving up the pretty French carriages of their masters, who have come to call on the ships' officers, or join in the general interest attending the arrival of one of their grand ships. Most of our passengers, I am sorry to say, have taken the cooler part of the day to take carriages and drive about to see the lions of the city; mostly zoölogical gardens. We can hear of no kind of a Protestant service anywhere. There is, however, a large Catholic cathedral here, and Catholic missions are pretty wide-spread in the province. However a miserable makeshift of a religion anywhere, it is especially abominable in heathendom, where it is not only tempted to compromise with heathenism and idolatry, but actually does it in the most open and monstrous manner.

Singapore. December 14.

If not exactly on the equator, we are only a degree and a half north of it. We reached here by the French Mail December 10, and found there was no steamer for Rangoon until the 15th (to-morrow). There was nothing to do but to wait, although at first I greatly regretted losing so much time that must be taken from Burma. Mr. W. concluded to take a steamer for Batavia, in the island of Java, thus crossing the equator, and seeing something of that wonderful place. It takes three days to go; accordingly he will not reach Burma till a fortnight after I do, so I remained here alone. I have, however, been much interested, and found the time none too long.

FAN PALMS.

This place is an English colony; i. e., the Island of Singapore, Penang and Malacca together are known as the Straits Settlement. This place is one of the greatest seaport exchanges or *entrepots* in the world. We see ships and people from all nations, — from England, Germany, France, Spain, Portugal, Australia, Borneo, Arabia, India, China, Japan, America, etc., — till one is bewildered in making them out. The street scenes, with people in all sorts of Eastern costumes, — Malaysian, Mohammedan, Bengali, Kling, Chinese, Tamil, etc., — are exceedingly picturesque and amusing. They are all tremendous traders; they dog your steps, haunt the verandas of your hotel, and pester you in your rooms, to buy jewelry, canes, shoes, white duck suits, silk fabrics, curios of every sort, or to ride in their queer little pony carriages, till you have to shake them off rather rudely at times to get rid of them. Yesterday a half-dozen of them beset me from the street, pushing their goods at me through the railing of the hotel veranda, where I sat drinking in the lovely tropical scenery and sniffing the sea breeze, which, though this is only a degree and a half from the equator, renders the climate here always the same and not very hot. The hotel clerk took pity on me, and rushed out of the office with a big squirt-gun filled with water, and gave the street venders a shower bath, much to my relief and their amusement. But it scattered them, and that sufficed.

VICTORIA REGIA.

American Methodist Mission.

I have found out some American Methodist Episcopal missionaries here, who have also a school of 400 Chinese boys (in English), and they have made me much at home, having me attend their semi-annual prize giving in the Town Hall, day before yesterday, at which the Governor presided, and also to dinner at the house of Mr. Munson, the principal, yesterday. There are several American teachers, and one from Prince Edward Island, a nephew of my friend Mr. D. of Charlottetown.

There are many very wealthy Chinese here, and some of them liberally favor the missions, and place their sons in the school. They raised $6,000, half the price of the school grounds, and presented it to the mission when they began, and they will do much more in the future. Many of them are millionnaires. Some of them have magnificent houses in European style, with spacious gardens and grounds, which all foreigners may inspect. I go to-morrow to see one of them. Chinamen nowhere in the world are so prosperous or so liberal-minded as here. Much is due to the just and wisely administered colonial government, under which they like to live, and where they make so much money in trade. There are over 100,000 Chinese on this small island, and millions more of them in the whole Malaysian Archipelago.

The hope of ultimately liberalizing and perhaps more rapidly Christianizing China proper is very large in this quarter, if Christian missions are worked as they ought to be hereabouts.

Mohammedanism.

These Malays, a people much blacker than other Asiatics I have seen, number in the whole archipelago 40,000,000, and they are (here, at least) all Mohammedans. Their mosques begin to appear. Of course in China there are many Mohammedans, though not near the coast, where I have been. Arriving here, the traveller realizes that a transition begins. And now all across Asia, westward from Singapore to Morocco, the Arab Mussulman will everywhere be seen. They are the most difficult of all non-Christian people to reach. There is scarcely a Malay Christian in Singapore. The London Missionary Society, which began a work among them here many years ago, gave it up through discouragement. Everybody among Mohammedans, whether rich or poor, counts it the most important thing in the world to go to Mecca.

MOHAMMEDAN MOSQUE.

There is one man here who is very rich. There are sixty acres in his grounds. He has his palace furnished in the costliest way imaginable. It is a museum of curios and rare treasures. He has plate of solid gold, many of the vessels being heavier than one could lift. Being a polygamist (as they all are), he has also houses and families in half a dozen countries, including India, Arabia and Turkey. On the day after Christmas he is to start from here on another pilgrimage to Mecca. He is to charter a German Lloyd steamer, and take 130 friends with him. What do you think of that for church going? If a man will do such things for a religion of superstition and sensuality, what should we not do for Christ's sake?

Multitudes of these people have also heard much of the gospel, so that they cannot plead ignorance; but they hate the gospel, the Bible, the very Christian name, and everything that rebukes their follies and sins. I have tried to converse with several Mohammedans, but their aversion to Christianity is something incredible to one who has not tested it. They say, "The Koran is a very good book, and Mohammed is the great prophet." The time will surely come when this power will be overthrown. Nothing but the spirit and power of God, however, is equal to it. At present the Chinese are much more easily reached than the Mohammedans.

SINEN, THE SUMATRAN TIGER KILLER.

To-morrow I expect to be on my way by the British India steamship "Puteali" to Rangoon, a five days' sail. Mr. Munson is going with me, and on to Calcutta, taking along one of his Chinese boys. The boy's father is wealthy, and is sending him out to see a little of the world.

One of these eleven-year-old lads in the school lately inherited $60,000. For all that, he still wears a pig-tail and yellow breeches as big as flour sacks. When he marched up to make his speech in behalf of the school to the governor at the prize giving, the other day, I noticed, however, that he had on a new unblacked pair of English shoes, which resounded through the hall like strokes of Thor's hammer, as he proudly walked. The speech, however, was in capital English, and showed decided talents. The Chinaman moves as well as other celestial bodies, especially in Singapore.

This morning I have promised to go with Mr. Kinsett, of the Methodist Episcopal Mission, to attend his Bible class of Chinese young men and talk to them a little. There is a fine young Siamese Baron, also a Christian, among them. I expect a good time.

A PLANTATION.

How I wish I could toss you and R. a bunch of bananas or mangos, or a lot of pineapples! They grow everywhere here. Bananas are worth only a cent a dozen. Wouldn't you feast on them if they were only that price at home? In a few days it will be Christmas. How different this tropical December weather from that in your frozen North! Well, I send you all wishes for the merriest sort of a time.

Penang.

S. S. "Puteali," PENANG HARBOR, December 17.

This morning found us in the harbor at Penang, 396 miles up the Straits of Malacca, north of Singapore. The place is an English settlement on a mountainous island, the island being only about fifteen miles long by twelve wide. The city may number perhaps 60,000 people, a couple of thousand being European. The balance are native Malays, Klings or Madras immigrants — who have come into the whole peninsula by thousands — and Chinese, the latter being, as usual, the most thrifty, pushing and wealthy of all. Many of these latter live like princes on fine estates. We went ashore for several hours, and took a drive five miles out to the waterfall, which also forms a small but lofty cascade running some hundreds of feet down the mountain-side. The drive was through the most thorough tropical scenery, embracing every variety of tree, shrub and foliage. The cocoanut palm especially abounds. There are miles of these orchards cultivated by planters, and looking up you can see great clusters of the ripening fruit hanging among the fronds. The commissioner of the public garden told us there were 4,000,000 fruit-bearing palms on the island alone; and across the strait in Wellesley Province, opposite, there are vast estates, producing not only cocoanuts, but sugar-cane, nutmegs, coffee, cloves, and other spices without limit. Pineapples, bananas, pomelos, mangos, mangosteens, etc., abound.

A JAVAN BOY.

Mr. Munson took me with him to call on the Bible Society colporter, Mr. Castells, a Spanish Methodist Episcopal brother; and who again should I find but another of Dr. Guinness' students, a friend of Upcraft's, and his young wife, just out to become married to him only two months ago, also a student for three years in Doric Lodge, and knowing well many of our English friends. They seemed pleased to see me, having read of me in *Regions Beyond*. Castells spoke particularly of his appreciation of my article on "Methods in Theological Education." He came out on the same steamer as far as Singapore with Miss Guinness. He then went for a while to the Philippine Islands. That being a Spanish colony and intensely Roman Catholic, he was arrested, imprisoned, and at last wholly driven out, and so was transferred to Penang. His companion, an old Spanish ex-priest, died in the islands, it is supposed from some foul play. Castells is a choice fellow, and doing a good work in Penang.

Equatorial Asia.

Nearing Burma.
December 19.

To-day we are lazily steaming along the Burman coast. We are not far from the latitude in which Judson was buried. We must now be about opposite Tavoy. The sea is like a mill pond for smoothness. All the morning we have been watching the flying fish, and more especially a vast shoal of some sort of larger fish, a mile away to our westward, which, from their antics, kept the sea in a boil along a stretch nearly ten miles in length. It was tremendous. (This is my biggest fish story yet.)

I confess to some impatience to get to Burma. I am much later than I hoped to be. Then the interest of the place is great, and the sentiment clustering about my thoughts of the historic spots is here at the maximum. We are aboard of a poor sort of a steamer of the British India Line. The cooking is abominable, especially in the second class, which I am taking on this trip to Calcutta, as I save thereby $30 to the Union. Besides, I think I ought to test the matter for myself, and see whether missionaries should really be encouraged to do this thing to save expense. My experience thus far is not reassuring in that direction, for which Messrs. Carpenter, Hudson Taylor and others plead. But I am resolved to be fortified on the point; at least, from actual experience of my own, when it is not too trying for health. When the seas are smooth, it is tolerable. The company is the most trying at times. At our table sit with us a German with a Burman

PAGODAS AT MAULMEIN.

wife, a Eurasian, four Chinese, three Americans, and a Scotchman. Our cooks and waiters are natives of India, exceedingly untidy,—Mohammedans,—and most of our passengers in the forward part of the ship, as well as all the crew, are likewise Mohammedans. Several of them have copies of the Koran in the Arabic, and frequently through the day they read aloud as orientals always read, in a monotonous and ear-distressing sing-song way. They are a dirty lot, and clad in old rags of garments, and meagre at that. Such are Asia, however, and the fruits of heathenism.

Under the Southern Cross.

Sunday Morning, December 21.

At 3 o'clock this morning we were awakened by the repeated monotonous call of the sailors outside, calling out their soundings in some barbarian tongue, "Panch bam, Panch ba-a-a-a-m, Achay Panch ba-a-a-m." That is "Five fathoms, five fathoms, five fathoms lacking one cubit," etc., indicating that we were approaching the Burman coast. We rose and took a look outside, which only revealed two distant coast lights, one being the light-ship. The silent stars were gleaming with wondrous brilliancy; except that at this hour the great Dipper, which in the early part of the night cannot be seen at all, it being below the horizon, was high towards the zenith, and turned bottom side up, as if too much disturbed to retain its contents. Besides this, many new constellations to the southward could be traced, including "The Southern Cross." We took in the silent, glittering majesty for a little, and retired to our bunk for another nap.

PAGODA, RANGOON.

Again at 6 o'clock we were roused by the soundings and the striking of the signal bells to the engineer to stop the ship. Looking out of our port to the eastward, the whole sky was aglow with the reddest dawn. We dressed and went on deck. We were lying close to "the pilot-brig," which is anchored in the roads outside the Rangoon River some twenty miles. A boat was being lowered from the brig, pulled by a half-dozen East Indian sailors, who brought a pilot to our ship's

Equatorial Asia.

side. He was an old man, seemingly seventy years of age, a thorough Englishman. He clambered up the ship's side on the rope ladder very feebly, as though he were about making port for the last time. Casting our eyes now to the northwest, we caught our first glimpse of the Burman coast, — a low, flat sand-bar line, stretching along the horizon for several miles, with a row of rather stately trees, dwindling on the left to something smaller, like low palms or brakes.

It was very tame and monotonous; as we expected, indeed, for south Burma is all flat and swampy. And yet as we sat there on deck in the cool morning breeze, watching the scene — which

PAGODA.

the sun, just rising fiery and glowing out of the sea, heightened to brilliancy and warmth, — thinking of what scenes have been enacted in the land lying beyond that coast line, and reflecting on what inspirations toward the furthering of Christ's kingdom in the earth have gone out from that little piece of oriental territory, the whole region thrilled with interest. I suppose that from no place in the wide world, except Palestine, have so many Christian inspirations been kindled as from the shores of Burma. Probably more young Christians have first or last become sensible of divine promptings to live unselfishly for human redemption on account of influence radiating from this new Holy Land than from any other profane country. Certainly this is so as regards the Baptist family, and I think as regards the Christian world at large. The thought that, God willing, in four short hours, I shall look upon Rangoon itself in the Sabbath light (for this is the Lord's day morning), and greet face to face on the spot some even of the veterans and associates of the Judsons, such as Mrs. Bennett, the Braytons and Mrs. Stevens, to say nothing of other heroes of a younger generation, fills me with awe and gratitude. I am to be permitted, if only for a little, to identify my person, my words, my prayers, my personal testimony, and my whole heart and life with the profound verities of this world-saving, heathen-dethroning movement of the ages. The moment when my feet shall press Burma's soil will be a lofty, thrilling and grateful moment to me. To engage this very day, as I hope to do, in the solemn services of God's house with native Karen and Burman believers in yonder city, beneath the very shadow of the departing memorials of heathenism, will not that be a feast to the soul of no common sort? My heart leaps in anticipation of the high festival!

We are now ascending the Rangoon River. In the distance, six or eight miles away, we catch a glimpse of the highest and most prominent object in the flat landscape; viz., the gilded pinnacle, with its h'tee, which crowns the Shwey Dagon Pagoda, emblem everywhere of heathenism, relic, doubtless, of the old Babel building, ever rearing itself in our sin-blighted world, and ever also, thank God, falling into ruins.

CHAPTER XIV.

On Burman Soil.

9 P.M.

WE landed at about 10.30 A.M. I was met by Mr. Miller of the Press, and driven to the home of Dr. Rose at Kemendine, a suburb of Rangoon, where I was most cordially received by the Roses and dear old Father Brayton, eighty-two years of age. Grandma Brayton, alas! to my deep disappointment, entered into rest last week, and was buried on Wednesday. She was a rare and saintly missionary, and passed away triumphantly. Thus sleeps in Burma's soil the dust of another of the martyr throng devoted to Burma's redemption.

After tiffin I went with Father Brayton, yet hale and vigorous after his fifty-three years of Burman toil, to the communion service for a group of Pwo Karen disciples in a chapel near by. It was touching to see and hear the ripe old patriarch, smiling and sunny through his tears, and despite his loneliness from his so recent bereavement, discoursing to the bright-faced company of natives, who sympathize with him so deeply, on "Jesus as the Resurrection and the Life." I partook of my first communion feast with these redeemed Karens. At the close, all gathered to shake hands with me. This afternoon Than Byah, a former student in America, came to call on me. He was so pleased to see me after twenty-three years. He and Brother S. spent a fortnight with me on the old Illinois farm during one of my college vacations. This evening I went to the Rangoon English church, to which Brother Whitman has just come to be pastor, and was thrust in to speak. I found a houseful. It seemed like America, with the fine large church, the nice looking people,—English, American and Eurasian, with occasional Karens,—the organ, chorus choir and all. I did not preach, but spoke familiarly of my errand, my observations in Japan and China, my pleasure at being in Burma, and the conditions of increased power all along the line. It is difficult to realize that I am really in this historic land. To-night I met young Professor Gilmore, at whose examination in Boston I was present in July. He comes from the West, and I from the East, having between us belted the globe.

December 25.

In Rangoon I am the guest chiefly of Dr. Rose, our capable and senior male missionary to the Burmans. His assiduous attentions, facilitating my various excursions through the country, lay me under much obligation. A most delightful reception, in behalf of all the missionaries, planned by the Roses, was given me at their house last evening. I was by no means a stranger there; most of those present were old friends. To-day I proceeded to Maulmein.

RANGOON BAPTIST CHURCH.

Visit to Maulmein.

I counted myself favored on this trip in having as my companion one of the real veterans in Burma, viz., Father Brayton. The dear man had only the previous Wednesday laid away all that was mortal of his beloved wife and companion in labors among the heathen for fifty-three years. Trying had been the ordeal, but God's grace had not failed. Full of praises to the goodness of the hand which so long had led him, out of a full and fresh memory of the beginnings of our work in this land, he vividly retraced for me the stages of its progress, and tenderly painted the personages which had prominently figured in it.

We took passage in the day steamer from Rangoon, which makes the run in about ten hours. These sped all too quickly, occupied, as they were, with reminiscences of the arrival on these shores of the fathers in the cause.

Our Glasgow-built steamer, coursing over the gulf of Martaban that day, seemed to live again with the presence of the devoted dead, as this one of the few contemporaries of Judson yet living in Burma, brought up before us the scenes which he had shared with Judson in village, zayat and jungle.

About 2 P.M. the long, low shore line of the Amherst district began to appear away to the eastward on our right. On yonder shore, just hard by the pagoda dimly seen rising from the rocks, rest the ashes of Ann Hasseltine Judson. We are disappointed not to be able to land; but the steamers do not now call here, so we must go on up the broad Salwen River twenty-five miles farther to Maulmein, and trust to some later opportunity to visit the hallowed spot.

On we steam; the mountains which rise loftily from behind and about Maulmein now begin to loom up to the north and westward; now great rice and lumber mills appear, with huge elephants handling teak logs and piling lumber in the yards along the river banks. The majestic cocoa palms adorn the slopes. Mammoth pagodas — some gray or green with age, some flashing golden and regal in the westering sunlight — crown all the heights.

On graceful undulating hillsides and terraces, amid gardens luxuriant with the tropical shrubs and foliage of this ever-green land, stand monasteries, mosques, government buildings, and houses — European and Burman, in endless variety. But amid and within the fascinating city, by no means large or populous, I discern what to me is of far more interest than them all; viz., the old Judson compound — the cradle of American Baptist missions, the spot on which the Burman Bible was translated and printed, and whence were written those letters, recording trials, disciplines and high ideals for the heathen, which have thrilled the church with a power scarcely less than that of the epistles of St. Paul. We are to visit that spot. Our blood leaps high with the enthusiasm of the hour. Maulmein is before us, beautiful, picturesque, historic and hallowed.

Our vessel draws up to her moorings. The docks are crowded with such a motley group of living creatures, — red-skirted Burmans, white-turbaned Tamils, Telugus and Klings from India, the ever-pushing, migrating, pig-tailed Chinaman, the shy, wild Shan, the Talign, the Arab and the Sikh. Pressing through the clamorous crowd, we now discern the figures of our two missionaries, Brethren Stevens and Armstrong, coming to take us off.

We are no sooner seated in the gharry (or pony cab) which is to drive us to Brother Stevens' house, than an old and wrinkled Burman woman draws near, and is introduced by Brother Stevens as one of the few living believers who were baptized by Dr. Judson. With an eagerness of interest for which we were unprepared, she thrust her withered hand through the gharry window; her moistened eye-lashes told of the feeling that ran deeply in her heart. She could

DR. JUDSON'S CHAPEL.

speak not a word of English, but we understood her. The chasm between foreign and home, between past and present, was that moment obliterated. We were face to face, hand in hand, eye to eye, and heart to heart, America and Burma, Judson's time and ours, in hand-clasp, in heart-union before the Lord. The Missionary Union in its representative was greeting one of its most distantly won trophies to the praise of our Lord's wondrous grace, on shores consecrated forevermore by the life and death of its first missionary.

We had not been a half-hour in Maulmein when, with Brother Stevens for guide, we had been shown over the old Judson and the Bennett compounds, where stands what is left (now enlarged into a building for a Burman boys' school) of the old first mission press, the Stevens compound, the Boardman place, and the premises of both the Burman and the English-speaking, semi-Eurasian church. Where the original Judson house once was, there is now only the green sward, with four frangipanni trees standing one at each corner of the place. One at least of these trees was planted by Judson's own hand. The fragrant blossoms loaded the early evening air with

PWO KAREN SCHOOL.

their delicate perfume While we stood and mused, a group of our bright school boys crossed the green and politely saluted us. Another group of children sat shyly but smilingly upon the curbstones about the old historic well at the corner of the Bennett house. Above the well rose the spreading branches of a majestic Amherstia tree, like another burning bush, with its long, scarlet, tasselly blossoms; while at the end of the long, narrow vista, which stretched down to the broad Salwen that flows at the foot of the garden, the western sky grew tender with evening blushes. The forms of stately palms which rose from the river banks pencilled their shadowy forms on the deep rich background of after-glow; and with our twilight musings, mingled with prayer for Burma's dark millions, the full realization was on us of the vast responsibility we inherit to carry on towards completion the work which the lofty spirits that have labored here inaugurated. May their God and His grace which proved sufficient for them be ours also.

In the evening of the day we first arrived at Maulmein, all our missionaries laboring there — a dozen strong — gave us a most cordial reception at the mission-house occupied by Mr. and Mrs. Bulkley, of the Pwo Karen Mission. Mr. Bulkley himself was out on a jungle tour of wide exploration among other Karen districts away eastward in Siam. The journey is made on elephants, and consumes weeks of travel.

The ladies in charge of the several schools in Maulmein — Burman, Karen and Eurasian — we found working with high enthusiasm, with difficulties by no means small.

It was a comfort to find that here Baptist work had become so prosperous as to require and necessitate establishments so large and commanding in influence as these.

Amherst and Mrs. Judson's Grave.

During the evening, arrangements had been perfected whereby, by spending the night aboard a native boat, we could be rowed by four oarsmen to Amherst, twenty-five miles distant, and visit the grave of Mrs. Judson. Brother Stevens and I went aboard at 11 o'clock, and at 7 o'clock the next morning we were awakened by the creak of the long sweeps of the rowers which drew us nigh to the rocky strand. Again we found a welcome awaiting us. A thoughtful Burman disciple at Maulmein had telegraphed some of the believers at Amherst; and standing on the rocks at the landing, with beaming faces underneath their yellow turbans, they saluted us as we approached. They had breakfast prepared for us at the old Haswell compound, — still occupied by Miss Susie Haswell, — and Mah-Theh-Oo waited to serve us. We needed no guide to find our way to the grave of Mrs. Judson. Scanning the rather low-lying sworded coast, which here rises only about thirty feet above the sea, almost the first object that arrested our eyes was a gray, once painted fence about a little clump of shrubbery situated only twenty-five feet from the sea, and standing quite alone on a clearing of several acres. No Hopia tree now stands above the place, although about 200 feet to the southward a noble specimen rises solitary and symmetrical against the sky. We made our way first to the grave itself, attended by a group of a half-dozen Burman sympathizers. Other groups of heathen soon gathered, and stood apart with wondering queries on their dark faces.

GRAVE OF MRS. JUDSON.

Within the little enclosure a dense growth of the shrub Lantana, now in blossom and very fragrant, completely covers the grave in which sleep the ashes of Mrs. Judson and her little Maria. At the head and foot of the grave, about which some brick-work is discernible underneath the shrubbery, there are two white marble slabs. On the headstone, beginning here and there to chip from exposure, we trace the inscription: —

Erected
To the memory of
ANN H. JUDSON,
wife of
Adoniram Judson, Missionary
of the
Baptist General Convention in the United States to the
Burman Empire.
She was born at Bradford,
in the State of
Massachusetts, North America,
Dec. 22, 1789.
She arrived with her husband at Rangoon in July, 1813,
and there commenced those Missionary Toils,
which she sustained with such Christian fortitude, decision
and perseverance amid scenes of civil commotion
and personal affliction, as won for her
universal respect and affection.
She died at Amherst
Oct. 24, 1826.

With no common interest did we here stand uncovered and read these words. In fellowship with the sufferings, both of the heroine who here sleeps and of the devoted husband who, returning from Ava, amid such disappointment, found his beloved wife, with her babe, buried from his sight forever, we lifted up voices of thanksgiving for such fortitude, and of prayer for the perpetuation of the sanctifying influence of such martyrs to world-wide evangelization. We plucked a few sprays from the shrubs which here were ever spring green and fragrant, and turned away girded with fresh devotion to this holy cause.*

The town of Amherst is a mere village of no commercial importance at all. We have here a little church. Among the members who gathered at the old Haswell house to greet us while we breakfasted, preparatory to our immediate return to Maulmein, was another old believer, Koo Lake by name, eighty-two years of age, baptized by Dr. Judson. Our kind hostess was Ma-Theh-Oo, who spent three years in America with Miss Haswell, now the wife of a worthy teacher in the old school at Amherst.

Returning early to Maulmein, we made rapid survey of all features and departments of our work. We met in the evening the members of the Burman church, about 200 strong; attended

* Since my visit to Amherst, on account of the encroachment of the sea, the grave has been removed to a spot many yards distant from the shore, and by the generosity of the Woman's Foreign Mission Society of Boston a neat iron fence has been erected around the new grave. These arrangements were carried out under the superintendence of Rev. W. F. Armstrong of Maulmein.

the English-speaking prayer meeting; were welcomed at a large social gathering given by Mr. and Mrs. Stuart, and were delighted to greet, among others, our old friend and brother, Dr. Shaw Loo, whom we had met in America in his student-days. We hear accounts of his extended usefulness in the pursuit of his profession. He superintends also the large Burman Sunday school.

Two days only could we devote to Maulmein, but they were high days of feasting along the line of some of the loftiest sentiments which from early childhood have grown strong within us.

LANDING ON THE IRRAWADDY.

The Bassein Mission.

What Maulmein and Rangoon have long been to work among the Burmans, that Bassein is to work among the Karens. Many early triumphs were won here. At all events, the fruits of those triumphs under the labors of Abbot, Beecher, Carpenter and others are clustered here. There are more than 8,000 Sgau Karen communicants connected with our churches in the Bassein district. Besides these, there are some 4,000 Pwo Karen communicants. Other important stations like Sandoway in Arracan and Henzada exist, which for lack of time we were regretfully unable to visit. What is to be seen at Bassein will suffice for a sample of the maturer results of work for the Karens.

Our trip was a twenty-four hours' sail by Irrawaddy steamer through various branches and creeks which compose the vast delta of the great river of Burma. The country is entirely flat, largely given to rice cultivation, although in some parts it is a densely wooded jungle. The

BURMAN MISSION-HOUSE.

banks of all the streams are of black mud, along which we see at intervals, sprawling in the sun, immense alligators, which at the blowing of our steam whistle or the report of a rifle, lumberingly wriggle off into the water. Two or three of our brother missionaries have joined us on the trip, to make the most of our time for a visit; and the good-natured, easy-going Bishop Strahan of Rangoon is also of our company.

I arrived at Bassein in the late afternoon, just before sunset. The prospect that lay before us was very winning. The tropical luxuriance of vegetation was something to remember; the gilded pagodas were flashing splendid in the sunlight, and the throng of gaily decked natives

KO-THAH-BYU MEMORIAL HALL.

about the wharves made a scene truly characteristic. As we disembarked and passed over the wharf to the long avenue which led up from the landing, our attention was directed to two companies of Karen young people grouped on each side of the avenue under the friendly palms. The one was a company of girls, and the other a company of young men from the schools, come out to meet us. A moment later, and Brother Nichols, with his black pony and American buggy, came driving down the avenue. He took us in, and we were driven up to the mission compound, a mile away, escorted by the smiling band of young people. On the way we passed the Burman mission-house and the headquarters of the Pwo Karen interest, consisting of two fine compounds with boys' and girls' schools, under the general direction of Brother L. W. Cronkhite, assisted by several ladies of the Woman's Board. Here we greeted former acquaintances in the

BASSEIN CHORAL SOCIETY.

West. Miss Higby and Miss Tschirch. We also passed the Burman chapel and compound, now, unhappily, without a missionary occupant, formerly occupied by the Jamesons. Grouped on the Sgau Karen compound, on high ground, are the mission-house built by the late Rev. J. S. Beecher (a brother-in-law of the writer), the Ko-Thah-Byu Memorial Hall, the girls' school, a hospital, and half a dozen boarding-cottages for students. It was an attractive prospect, and showed evidences of thrift and good management on every hand.

There was a pleasant sense of being at home as we were ushered into the rooms in the mission-house, for years occupied by those closely bound to us by family ties. We found the Beechers were warmly remembered by multitudes of the people, including teachers and preachers of two generations. Mr. Beecher came to this field in 1846, making his first voyage to Burma in company with Dr. Judson, who then made his last. Mr. Beecher labored here for nineteen years.

His practical stamp is on many of the workers. He rests from his labors in Plymouth, England, and his works do follow him.

There were three notable gatherings of all branches of the mission during our two days' sojurn. Two of these were in the Ko-Thah-Byu Memorial Hall, on which occasions we had the pleasure of addressing three or four hundred of the Karens, mostly pupils in the schools. The third occasion was at the dedication of the new Pwo girls' school building. It was a spectacle to see these assemblages of bright, intelligent youth, trophies of gospel influence. Their appearance was very picturesque, in their pink turbans, white jackets, and bright colored skirts, and how they did sing! A choir of about fifty of them treated us to a concert, rendering some of the finest choruses from classic composers as Abt, Mendelssohn, etc., with English words, which truly astonished us. That same choral society was practicing on the "Messiah" by Handel, expecting soon to give it before the Chief Commissioner of Burma and the elite of Rangoon, as they had previously rendered other compositions in elaborate concerts. Besides this, the young men have a brass band, using a score or so of instruments. Dressed in their European uniforms, they presented a fine appearance, and discoursed sweet strains for us during part of one afternoon.

DA BUH.

PADDY BIN.

Nothing moved me more than the dozen or more veteran preachers who had come in from various parts of the jungle to present their salutations. Among them was one old man of tall figure and large brain, Myat-Keh by name, ninety years of age. He was one of the early converts. I think he was a survivor of one of those companies of Karens who in the early days came in over the Arakan hills by midnight, for fear of their Burman oppressors by day, to hear the gospel at Abbot's eloquent lips and to receive baptism. At the close of my address on the second evening, Myat-Keh was called out in response, and spoke most fervently, the address being interpreted for me into English. Other interesting characters were introduced to me, such as Yah-ba and Myah-sa, doing valuable work in the schools. Then there was Da-Buh, the well-to-do and devoted deacon who is so eager an evangelist to the Karen people that he sends out, from time to time, at his own expense, evangelizing expeditions to distant tribes, as in Northern Siam, with the gospel tidings.

Another special feature of the work at Bassein which impressed us was the industrial enterprise in the form of a large lumber mill, on the bank of the river, which the Karens have purchased and are successfully operating. There were gang saws at work cutting teak timber; "Diston

GIRLS' SCHOOL.

saws" from Philadelphia; "Rogers' planers" were in operation; sash and doors were making. All of this was entirely carried on by the Karens. There was a Karen superintendent, a Karen book-keeper, and a Karen in charge of the engine; and down at the landing another Karen engineer and a pilot, to manage Brother Nichols' steam launch as he goes up and down the rivers touring among the jungle churches.

The Karens have also an artificial ice-making establishment; they have their own rice mills; they have an extensive printing-establishment; they make their own hymn books, etc. Self-support has reached a high state of development in the Bassein Mission, as all the world knows through Mr. Carpenter's writings. Missions like this are anything but a failure. The Missionary Union, moreover, is most fortunate in the present able management of the Bassein work under Messrs. Nichols and Cronkhite. They have been thus fortunate on this field from the beginning. Here, surely, if anywhere on Asiatic mission-fields, is a miracle of missionary success.

On the return to Rangoon, we had a bare glimpse of Maubin by lamplight and at midnight; of the external features of the admirable work for Pwo Karens at Maubin, under the conduct of Mr. and Mrs. Bushell, assisted by Miss Putnam. The captain detained the steamer for an hour in the night watches, to allow us this brief call. At Waukema, also *en route*, the steamer lay to for an hour, while we visited the mission-house lately vacated by the devoted Jamesons. Here we saw the Sunday school in session, and met several capable native workers. When the children were asked if they would like to send greetings to the American children on the other side of the world, they were silent; but when asked if they " knew Teacher Jameson," and would like to send their love to him, they all promptly sprang to their feet. Alas! that so often in stations like this, when the worn-out missionary is compelled to go home to recruit, there is no one prepared to take his place, and so for years the work languishes or devouring wolves come in and spoil the flock.

The Burman State Railway.

When Judson visited Ava from Rangoon, in 1824, he was six tedious weeks in making the up-river voyage of 350 miles by native boat. We made the trip, taking the Burman State Railway, in twenty-two hours. The Burma of to-day, as a well-regulated British province, is anything but the Burma of 1824. You board the train at Rangoon, and roll out of a modern station having all the appearance and convenience of a western railway centre; and from thence, on to Mandalay, you pass through numerous station towns attended with all the bustle and business that characterize a trunk line in the western states of

PLOWING RICE-FIELDS.

America. Many new and flourishing towns, like Yemethen and Pyinmana, are springing up, which give promise of new enterprises, and involve the shifting of population from old centres, precisely as a railway line in Dakota or Kansas reconstructs the life of a piece of American territory. Modern enterprise is by no means confined to the Occident. The Orient is pulsating also with the world-thrill of human and divine action. Burman plains, mountains and jungles, as really as American pampas, are being populated by restless peoples who, from China, India and other over-peopled regions, seek the virgin tracts which, in Burma, are being reclaimed from wild beasts and wilder jungle wastes.

The Burman railway, for the whole 350 miles, runs through a comparatively level region. In the southern part you pass through a vast stretch of rice-fields, that in appearance are much like the old-time stubble-fields of Illinois when it was a wheat-growing state. In the northern part, the lands are less fertile, often alkaline, resembling Nebraska plains, except that occasional palms and groves of scrubby timber spring up through the dry and sunburned landscape. Away

LIFE OUT OF DEATH.

to the eastward, paralleling the line of railway, a lofty range of evergreen mountains stretches the whole distance. To the westward, may be seen lower undulating slopes and elevations, beyond which flows the turbid Irrawaddy.

During the last seventy-five miles of the journey nearing Mandalay, we approach close to the eastern hills. We meet with more abundant water supply and with increased beauty of hill scenery. We discern also, alas! as in all heathen countries, the multiplied emblems of idolatry. Pagodas crown all the hilltops, frequently the very hillocks and even isolated rocks, sometimes a score in a group. In some cases a hundred or so are clustered picturesquely within a diameter of a mile. We are reminded by these thronging emblems that we are nearing the very seat of Buddhism in Burma for nearly 900 years, as well as the historic seat of Burma's idolatrous royalty, established successively by various proud monarchs at Amarapoora, then at Ava, and finally at Mandalay, where Thibaw recently surrendered almost without a show of resistance. These three cities (only the ruins of the two former remaining to be seen) are all situated within a diameter of about ten miles. As our train rolls on, we find ourselves moving through extensive ruins of the environs of Amarapoora. Now we dash through the remains of an ancient wall made of bricks, some thirty feet in thickness and twenty feet in height. Ruins of temples, monuments and monasteries are strewn on every hand. There stands a Buddha cleft clean down the back by the stroke of time; and the lofty zayat, which has long sheltered it, looks as if the next train that thundered past would topple it over. "O shade of Ah rah-han (the first Buddhist apostle of Burma)! weep over thy falling fanes! retire from the scenes of thy past greatness! But thou smilest at my feeble voice. Linger there thy little remaining day. A voice mightier than mine, a still small voice, will ere long sweep away every vestige of thy dominion. The churches of Jesus will soon supplant these idolatrous monuments, and the chanting of the devotees of Buddha will die away before the Christian hymn of praise." Thus exclaimed Judson, as in 1824 he surveyed the 999 pagodas of Pagan, not far from this same region. Thus we say to-day, with the multiplied tokens of God's breath of indignation scattering to the plains the dust of these crumbling piles.

Mandalay.

Arrived at the station in Mandalay, Brethren Kelly and Sutherland met us, and we were soon resting on the broad veranda of Brother Kelly's mission-house. Dr. Packer of Meiktila had joined us on the way; and some eight or ten other missionaries from the vicinity, including two ladies from Maulmein, on a visit, soon gathered, and in the evening we had a conference, clos-

MANDALAY.

ing with much fervent prayer for God's special blessing on this new, yet old, centre of work in Upper Burma. There are five bases of operation for work among Burmans in and near Mandalay: Mr. Kelly's mission compound, including a girls' school; the Judson Memorial Church compound, including the fine new brick church; a teak school building and a new brick school building just rising; the new mission-house, within the walls of the city proper, occupied by Mrs. Hancock; the day school building, in a thronged quarter of the city, and the fine compound occupied by Mr. and Mrs. Sutherland, at Sagaing, sixteen miles down the river.

Mandalay, with its population of 200,000, is strategically the most important centre, if we seek Burman conversion in the whole empire. Judson knew it from the beginning. An awful chasm had to be crossed to reach it, — broader than even he knew, — but we have reached it at last, thanks to God's providence, painful and slow though it has been, and right ably is it being occupied, as respects the character of the devoted men and women now in possession.

Ava, the Golden.

The morning of our second day in this region we devoted to a trip down the river by steamer to Sagaing and old Ava, "the golden." Sagaing is now the principal town, the residence of a deputy commissioner, and an

SAGAING.

important railway station on a new line. It is beautiful for situation, occupying a dense grove of tamarind trees, and surrounded by lofty promontories, crowned with pagodas and kyoungs of myriad numbers and forms — the creations of past dynasties, which would fain pile up merit through these artistic accumulations of whitewashed bricks, with gilded h'tees tinkling with bells by the thousand.

What was once Ava lies directly opposite Sagaing. The Irrawaddy is here three fourths of a mile wide. A dismantled wall skirts the bluff above the river-bed for miles. When Mandalay was built, the capital of the former monarch was destroyed; and so the city which Judson saw formally occupied with so much pageantry and circumstance that he declared it " far surpassed anything he had ever seen or imagined," is now, and long has been, not only wholly a ruin, but the very grounds on which the city stood have become a jungle of tangled tropical shrubbery and vines. A few squatter villages are sprinkled through the place. There are ruins of a few monasteries and pagodas; while of the splendid new palace of Judson's time, only the tall, square-built bell tower remains, and that is leaning to a speedy fall. It is picturesquely covered with vines. The belfry, whence the Judsons heard strike the dismal hours of their long-drawn agony, is now the home of bats and lizards. The place is death-struck, and one cannot resist the impression that the woe of God overtook the place; while, as a sturdy old Burman said, at our farewell meeting in Rangoon, "The region near where Judson suffered, has been made an honorable place to Judson's renown, by the erection of the Memorial Chapel."

A worthy Burman pastor, who knew the site of the old "Death Prison," was our guide to the

BELL TOWER OF AVA.

spot. It was nearly two miles from where the Judsons lived, about a quarter of a mile from the palace tower. There is only a heap of rubbish, amid which we found a little white marble elephant, symbol of departed royalty, to mark the spot. Two stately trees overshadow it.

Beneath their shade, our party gathered, sang "Jesus shall reign where'er the sun," and then Dr. Packer led us in prayer for a new baptism of power on all workers for Burma. The native pastor followed in a pathetic petition for the same blessing. We refreshed ourselves from our lunch baskets, chatted with the poor straggling natives, who curiously hung about us, climbed the crumbling steps to a great shrine which once overlooked the prison, but which now is rotten with age and neglect, and came away in good mood for the reception given us by the native church, at the Memorial Chapel compound, in the afternoon and evening.

SITE OF THE DEATH PRISON.

Judson Memorial Chapel.

Delightful as all these meetings with the Karen and Burman Christians have been, none came nearer to our hearts than this one. First, we were served to tea; then we were introduced to a score or so of veteran pastors and teachers, including one old, blind deacon, a disciple of Kincaid.

Then came a detachment of eighty uniformed Karen policemen, all Christians, in the employ of the government. There is a battalion of these, 400 strong. Then the hand-shaking began. We adjourned from the schoolroom to the chapel, and after Scripture, hymns and prayer, we addressed them. Brother Kelly interpreted. It must have been with rare skill and with a full heart; it surely was magnetic upon both speaker and audience. The episode of the morning had brought to us almost the companionship and spiritual presences of the mighty sufferers of Ava and Oung-pen-la. We began with allusions to the high interest of the locality, then passed on

JUDSON MEMORIAL CHURCH.

to the power of the cross principle, and the need of it in all our work. The Spirit honored it. It was evident to all, as we sat there in the twilight, — to the Karens who sat tearful on the right, to the Burmans whose flashing eyes responded on the left, to the dear missionaries who yearned and sympathized in front, — that God was near. It was suggested that we close with a prayer and consecration meeting in front of the pulpit. Scores, both of Karens and Burmans, pressed forward. For a half-hour prayer flowed, all of us on bended knees, especially that new power might be poured on all for Burman evangelization. It was a melting time. It was good to be there. One Karen youth pressed forward at the close to say, with moistened eyes, that he "meant to be faithful unto death." Several Burman young women testified to marked blessing received. God give it permanence and power, that we may begin to see among Burmans what we have long seen among Karens!

Oung-pen-la.

The next morning, a party of a dozen of us, including several of the Burmans whose hearts had been so warmed the evening before, drove to Oung-pen-la, distant from Mandalay four miles. The present place is a squalid little village of perhaps thirty houses. The site of

DEDICATION DAY AT MEMORIAL CHURCH.

the old prison is a vacant lot, hard by a little kyoung and another decaying pagoda. The paddy bins, the quaint old ox carts with plank wheels and wooden axles, precisely like those Mrs. Judson describes as used by her in the rides to and from Amarapoora across the dry, hot plain, were there to be seen. We recalled the pathetic scenes and experiences which her graphic pen describes. We thanked God that those sufferings long ago were ended, and for their awakening effect on the American church, and for the prospect Brother Kelly says there is, that on this very mission ground a Baptist Christian chapel may soon be built. Again, under the shade of the neighboring trees, we gathered for a little prayer and praise meeting, some engaging in English and some in Burman, the groups of village children and others lingering near with wondering eyes. For them also we prayed, and for their descendants to latest time, that they might know Him for whose sake the early sufferers on this spot lived and died.

SITE OF PRISON PEN, OUNG-PEN-LA.

A Karen Association.

January 15.

It was a most favoring providence that timed the meeting of one of our Karen associations so as to exactly correspond with the week we had to devote to Central Burma. Dr. Bunker of Toungoo was on the lookout; and one morning, just as we were despairing of such a coincidence, he overtook us ten minutes prior to sailing for Maulmein, and persuasively outlined to us his anticipations in our behalf. These, in brief, were that we should go out with him and a half-dozen other missionaries two days' journey from Toungoo, eastward, over two ranges of mountains, and attend the annual associational gathering of about sixty or more of the B'ghai Karen churches.

SHAN MISSION-HOUSE, TOUNGOO.

It would involve some hard climbing over mountain bridle-paths, with some camping out amid the wilds of the jungle, with some exposures. But what were these compared with an opportunity to see the Burman jungle in all its wild variety, to observe the Karen in his primitive villages and mountain haunts, with five days of intercourse with the missionary brethren and sisters on the veritable field, face to face with the conditions under which jungle work is carried on, and face to face, also, with a blessed sphere of influence, which none who have not witnessed it can ever realize. Here was an opportunity to go along and sample the thing for ourselves. We resolved that to put in one week, out of three in Burma, in the jungle itself, was the wisest economy of time, whatever mere stations with comparative comforts and interests should appear neglected.

On Monday morning, after the Sabbath spent at Toungoo, in pleasant converse with the Crosses, Johnsons, Cochranes, Kirkpatricks, Dr. Cushing and others, we started: four missionaries, two American visitors, several boys, two cooks, fourteen coolies, four ponies, and two elephants bearing our camping outfit, provisions, etc. For a couple of hours we threaded our way along a dusty path through the high reeds and tiger-grass which abound upon the wide stretch of the river bottom-lands. Later we found ourselves astray in a by-path which wandered into a dense government preserve of teak forest, the most valued wood of Burma. We recovered our bearings, and rose to the foothills of the first range of mountains. Now forest trees began to appear, of large diameter, rising sheer without a branch for 100 feet, and then spreading into a broad, rich canopy top. What roots they have! shooting out in great fan-shaped buttresses, starting often from twenty feet above the ground, bracing the trees on every side. These are oil trees, and there are many banyans with such net-works of branches running downward as well as upward. Then note the vines, twisted, gnarled, knotted and often binding together a dozen trees, as if throttling a squad of them to the death. The thorny-barked rattan depends on every side; clumps of bamboo, in scores of species, stand thick about us, and palms many and picturesque. The curious nest of the weaver bird tempts us aside, in a vain attempt to reach the coveted prize. The stillness is as solemn as the tropical monarchs are majestic. Anon we come upon mountain brooks, babbling and musical as a Vermont trout stream. Often the jungle is so tangled that we are compelled to make our way up the bed of a stream; then our ponies, clambering up the rocky banks, tug for hours up a rugged bridle-path to some great height, whereon we find a lookout over a wide landscape of wondrous loveliness.

A JUNGLE PROCESSION.

Towards the end of the first day, while we are resting for a little by a singing, cool brook, we hear the "tunk-a-tunk" of an elephant bell, and a few minutes later, issuing from the copse that overhangs a dry ravine, a great "Jumbo" appears, packed and girded, with a Karen on his neck, a group of half a dozen others following. This company proves to be one of our village pastors, with several other delegates, on their way, likewise to the association. There in the wilderness the introductions with the hand-shakings began, and for four days they went on with scarcely any cessation. The Karens we found to be great hand-shakers. This new company now became our guides to the village, two hours farther on, where we were to encamp for the night. On they led us, through tangled ways, around shoulders of the cliffs, down through ravines, across rice-fields, under overhanging bamboo groves, till at length, just at dusk, we arrived at the entrance to a village, situated in a most secluded retreat.

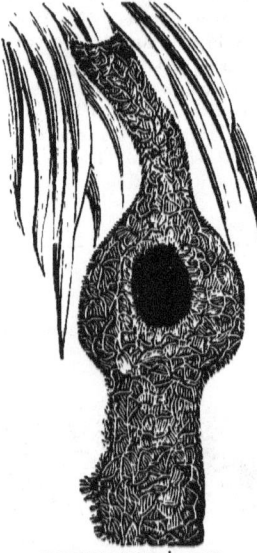

WEAVER BIRDS' NEST.

It seems we had been expected. What preparations they had made for us! By what system of telegraphy I know not, but somehow, from the moment Dr. Bunker sent out the word that we were to come, the whole jungle, through a wide district, dotted by half a hundred villages, became aware of it, and Karendom was at our service and on the watch towers for our humble coming. At this village of our right halt, apparently men had been at work for days preparing for our arrival and comfort. They had constructed booths and booths: two large ones, with floors well elevated above ground, with roofs, and walls at the sides, and even steps, with a hand-rail for safe ascent. On the floors of these booths, all of split and woven bamboo, everything constructed without nails, we were to pitch our tents and spread our beds. A cooking-booth was also prepared, and a neat and ingenious woven bamboo table. Wood had been gathered for our fires, and water brought in bamboo buckets for ourselves and our beasts. Without a match or a flint, the Karens lighted our fires; all with that magical bamboo. They brought fowls for our meal, and, with a round of hand-shaking that betokened fellowship of the genuine sort, they bade us welcome to their best. A couple of hours afterwards they joined us around the campfire at our evening worship. It was solemn and touching, there in the moonlight, our fires brightly blazing, the elephants and ponies browsing among the herbage near by, to witness the kneeling company, listen to the voices of prayer, now in English and now in Karen, and to hear from all the Karens the "Amen" at the close. As our evening song floated above the trees, we thought of far-distant friends in America, whose loving prayers have followed us even to these wilds.

"Though sundered far, by faith we meet
Around one common mercy-seat."

At daybreak of the second day, we had broken camp, and were again on the march, up and ever up the mountain slopes, with occasional crossings of the mountain streams, and with more numerous meetings with the highland villages. In each of these settlements there was a chapel, by far the best building in the place. There were the worn Karen Bible and hymn book on the bamboo desk. Each evening in all these Christian villages where there is a teacher, as is usually the case, it is the custom for the teacher to gather the whole community for evening Scripture reading, explanation, singing and worship. In one of these evening services which we attended on our return, we counted sixty-five present. They were poor, so poor in appearance! not unlike the Indians of the American border; but they heard a clear exposition of precious divine truth. They knew and sang, "Thus far the Lord hath led me on," and in prayer all were on their faces before God. In communities like these, to be found by the score, is the place, by the way, to observe the fruits and value of the *school* work, often narrowly criticised, which goes on in places like Maulmein and Bassein. Without teachers trained in just such schools, there could be no such influences kept perpetually working in numerous far-out jungle villages in Burma.

The missionaries at the best can be only field marshals over the churches, directing these native country teachers trained by the school, and set to work out the details in behalf of native populations.

About 5 o'clock in the afternoon of the second day, as we came around on a sort of high, curved water shed of the range of hills we had for hours been ascending, we entered a piece of cleared ground, amid which was a native cemetery. There were

KAREN JUNGLE VILLAGE.

monuments of bamboo and boards raised to a few of the believers who had passed away, with touching allusion in the inscriptions to their blessed exchange of worlds. We were on the confines of the settlement wherein the associational meeting was to be held. Casting our eyes now across the deep valley to the right, we saw, lying on a bold promontory a mile away, like an islet amid a sea of valleys, with a lofty range filling the deep background twenty miles beyond, the village which was waiting to receive us.

A moment more, and a company of brethren came to escort us in. Arrived at the place, what interest we felt in each scene! There was Brother Crumb, over from another mountain district, in which he had been touring for two months among the Paku Karens, come to meet us. Three sisters had also come in from their jungle travels to join in the meeting; viz., Miss Simons, Miss Ambrose and Miss Anderson, the latter from our own dear Minnesota. Here again we found the natives had fairly built a small town of booths and houses for all sorts of uses for our comfort. What a tabernacle they had prepared for the meetings! It reminded us of the old days of the mammoth Moody tabernacles, except — well, it didn't cost $30,000. It was only bamboo and thatch. There was a carpet of bamboo, on which the 1,058 delegates from fifty-six villages and churches sat. There was a high pulpit and an elevation for the dignitaries, a table for the scribes, and a place for the half-dozen or more choirs, from as many different districts, that so charmingly sang. Here again appear the fruits of your lower Burma schools. Rills of numberless good things permeate these wild and half-barbarous jungles like streams from Paradise, and are starting in this wide wilderness the beginnings of the new Eden.

Through two evening sessions and a whole day we sat and drank in the proceedings. An able Karen presided. In his prayer, which concluded the associational gathering, he addressed the Lord as follows, respecting my visit: "And now, Lord, we have seen the great Secretary of the great Missionary Union! and we see that he is neither a giant nor an animal nor a griffin, but *only a man* like ourselves. So we shall have to continue trusting Thee for all our needs just as we have been doing heretofore." A pretty sensible disciple that, we all concluded.

The giving was an astonishment to us, considering the universal poverty of these hill peoples. They have no industries as yet in these remote parts. There is a crying need for industrial teachers. It is surprising and startling to see, after all, how little has been accomplished when these peoples who, when they do accept the gospel, come in by whole villages, are simply evangelized. They have accepted Christ, the Bible, the hymn book, the missionary and the village teacher, but for a long time they remain still in ignorance, in filth, in much real social degradation. They need to be inducted into the elements of a Christian civilization as well.

At the afternoon service the representative of the Missionary Union was received by the association. Their enthusiasm and gratitude were touching; their appreciation of what was said to them, gratifying. It was especially interesting to see the influence over them of their missionaries, whom they revere almost as gods. What bishoprics are here! The Missionary Union is especially fortunate in that for more than twenty years — years in which the whole mission, centering at Toungoo, was at one time threatened with wholesale disaster — there have been in charge such men as the now venerable Dr. Cross among the Pakus and Dr. Bunker among the B'ghais. Lost ground has been steadily recovered and rapid gains made, despite a form of ritualistic proselytism which the missionaries have had to contend against, that is as cruel as it is shameless and unprincipled.

On the morning of the third day we broke camp, Dr. Bunker, Brother Crumb and the lady missionaries, attended by several of the experienced school girls, pushing out into regions beyond, for their annual visitation of the churches, while we returned to Toungoo. "It takes pluck to do that," remarked a new missionary of our company just out from home, as he saw Miss Simons mount her packed elephant next morning and leave us, accompanied by her Karen assistants and the coolies, for a plunge into deeper jungles for two months more of visitation among the churches before the rains begin. Such work as this all these brave young women are doing. O ye luxury-loving daughters in America, could ye endure a test like this to prove your love to Christ and immortal souls? And yet believe me, these devoted workers ask not for your commiseration. They prefer these toils, even with all their exposures, to any prizes which this world can offer. They simply ask for your prayers and co-operation.

Among the red-letter days of a lifetime, we have entered high up on the calendar the days spent in the B'ghai Karen district contiguous to Toungoo.

Our Shan Mission.

In connection with our visit to Toungoo, we came into touch with our Shan Mission — first, through the companionship of Dr. J. N. Cushing, our senior missionary to the Shans, and the able translator of their Scriptures ; secondly, through our visit to the old Shan mission-house at Toungoo, where we saw somewhat of the work as it is carried on among a limited number of these people who frequent such stations as Toungoo and Mandalay ; and thirdly, through the meeting with Drs. Kirkpatrick and Griggs, who had, by forced marches from Thibaw, managed to reach Toungoo for an interview before we left. Mr. W. W. Cochrane, also designated to work among the Shans at Bhamo, was temporarily located at Toungoo. Dr. Cushing has high hopes for these interesting people, and earnestly pleads for young men to occupy commanding points in their territory, such as Moné. We heard also from the lips of Dr. Kirkpatrick encouraging accounts of the favor he had found from the authorities and people at Thibaw, where new mission-houses are building. Dr. Kirkpatrick placed in our hands an interesting souvenir in the way of a fine wild peacock's tail, given him by a Shan, who, while on his way to present it to a Buddhist priest, fell in with a copy of the Gospel of John, distributed by our workers, and concluded that he would make no more gifts to the priests. He became convinced, after sitting up most of the night to read the new book, that it was true. He accordingly brought the peacock's tail to our missionary, instead of to the priest.

Pegu.

At Pegu, on the arrival of the train, I was met at 3 o'clock A.M. by Miss Payne, taken in her pony phaeton, and driven away to the mission compound, a mile and a half distant. In the morning I was shown her dove cote of a mission-house, the tidy Burman chapel, her enterprising reading-room, just at the end of the bridge, on the main thoroughfare of the city, and introduced to some of the most intelligent Christian Burmans I had the pleasure of meeting anywhere. Her thrifty school pleased me greatly. This sister is the sole missionary in charge at this station. According to the testimony of the deputy commissioner of Pegu, whom I met later in the day "She is a captain of every good work in the town."

CHAPTER XV.

Three Veterans.

RANGOON, December 27.

AMONG the peculiar satisfactions which came to me in my visit to Burma, were the meetings with veterans who have been upon the field over fifty years. These persons were Rev. D. L. Brayton, Mrs. Cephas Bennett and Mrs. Dr. E. A. Stevens. They were all contemporaries with Judson during the latter period of his life, were intimately associated with him, and partook deeply of his spirit.

Rev. D. L. Brayton.

My interview with Father Brayton on the trip to Maulmein, before referred to, during two full days, gave me the most favorable opportunity to gather some of his more striking reminiscences. The Braytons sailed from Boston October 28, 1837, on the bark "Rosabella," a vessel of 300 tons. Five months afterwards they arrived at Amherst. The Stevenses and Stillsons sailed at the same time. Brother Haswell met them on arrival. Soon after, Osgood and Judson came to meet them. "Judson had piercing eyes, and was a man capable of severity. . . . The ship on which we came brought the paper for the first edition of his Burman Bible." Referring to the frequent allusions made in letters from home to the trials of a missionary's life, Mr. Brayton said : —

"Tell them to talk not of trials ; talk of privileges. Think of what it is to see the dark countenance of a heathen light up — a joy the world knows nothing about. Don't mention sacrifices ; they are not worth talking about. . . . Judson never said a word about sufferings unless drawn out, and then he would check and rebuke himself. . . . I was associated with Judson for thirteen years."

Dr. Brayton's account of his jungle tours, accompanied by his devoted wife, and the eagerness with which the poor people would cluster about their boat or zayat to hear them explain the good news contained in the "White Book," was most touching. Sometimes a poor old woman would come and inquire "If there was anything in the White Book to cure the sorrows of the heart."

He mentioned one man whose wife and family opposed his becoming a Christian. They had prepared a feast to cheer up the husband and father from the melancholy brought on by his conviction. At length, because he would not eat of the feast, his family forsook him, saying, "You'll not see our faces again." "Very well," said he, "I must eat rice for myself." He was baptized, and proved true. Villages sent invitations to the missionaries to come and explain to them the book, and prepared lodgings for them. They went, and great salvation was wrought. "For thirty-five years," said the veteran, "our life was filled up with such experiences." Still, the eagerness for the work and joy in it are unabated. The fire of a war horse is in him still, rising daily at 4 o'clock in the morning to toil upon his revision of the Pwo Karen Bible.

Mrs. Bennett.

MRS. BENNETT.

It was my pleasure to spend a forenoon in the home of Mrs. Bennett. Although in her eighty-third year, this sister is yet so vigorous that she daily performs much mission work. Her house is constantly frequented by the Burman women and girls, and by native preachers and missionaries, consulting her on all sorts of matters. Her mental vigor is such that she is able to impart most valued counsel. Her native wards are numerous; they look to "Mamma Bennett" as to no one else.* On Christmas Day she was able to go into the town and attend a Christmas-tree exercise for the children in a Eurasian school, entering into it with the zest of a woman in middle life. In the course of our conversations, I noted down the following items from her fund of reminiscences:—

"We were appointed missionaries of the Union in 1828. We left the capes of the Delaware in the brig 'Mary,' for Calcutta, the 8th of September, 1830. . . . My husband was the eldest son of Rev. Alfred Bennett of Homer, N.Y. He was a printer; formerly publisher of the *Baptist Register*, since developed by Dr. Edward Bright into the *Examiner*. We first landed in Burma at Amherst. Judson had taken up his residence at Maulmein; he was living with the Wades. The Boardmans had gone to Tavoy. In going from Amherst to Maulmein, we were rowed the whole distance of twenty-five miles in an open boat. We arrived at 8 o'clock in the evening. Judson was a rather dignified character, and did not come to the landing to meet us, but sent a Eurasian to conduct us to his house, who also carried the baby. Arriving at the compound, we found the missionary living in a bamboo house, with a bamboo floor, standing high up on bamboo posts. We were made quite welcome. We had brought out the presses with us for the printing of the Burman Bible. A month after our arrival, Dr. Judson, who was then in his first widowhood, came and boarded with us for three years. This, of course, brought us into very close contact with him. He was reserved, very methodical in his work, precise in his attire, and particular about his wardrobe. He was very fond of early morning walks, often rising unseasonably early and going over the hilltops, where he was exposed to the danger of being seized by tigers; but he was perfectly fearless, and hard to change from his course. The native church now numbered about thirty members of

---

* This mother in Israel has since passed away.

Burmans and Taligns, who had removed to Maulmein from Rangoon and Dalla, to get away from persecution. These disciples were gathered by Judson at the mission-house every evening for prayer and instruction. These were times of great rejoicing in those otherwise dark days. Some of the native Christians developed strongly. Such were Ko Shwey-ba and Ma Doke. Then we began to live. Judson was then at work upon his translation of the Bible. On one occasion he got me to count the verses from Isaiah to Malachi, that he might know how many verses to translate per day in order to finish his work by a given time. He was very domestic in his feelings, and particularly fond of children. He would sit on the floor and play with them, caress their dolls, and sing lullabies to them. Friends counselled him to remarry, but he would not hear a word to it, so long as his Bible was unfinished. This done, he went away to Tavoy without saying a word to any of the missionaries, and married Mrs. Boardman, making a confidant only of Mr. Blundell, the British commissioner; brought his bride back to Maulmein, and for a time they both boarded with me."

The time soon came when Mrs. Bennett's two children were to be sent home. The mother sat in her room weeping at the separation, when a letter from Dr. Judson, full of tenderness and sympathy, was put into her hand. This ripe worker, after sixty-two years of service on Burman soil, was alive with fresh suggestions as to present-day needs. She had much to say concerning the character of seminary training of our native preachers. She pleaded that our management should not continue to place so great responsibility upon single women at the head of the largest schools, but that we should place a man and his wife in such positions. She seemed to have clear apprehensions of the work going on, especially in the Burman department. She would not have less work done for the Karens, but far more for the Burmans. She spoke on all these themes with the force and fervor of a prophetess.

Mrs. Stevens.

The last of the trio who have labored above fifty years on Burman soil is Mrs. Dr. Stevens. Her home is with her son-in-law, Rev. D. A. W. Smith, D. D., at Insein, the pretty suburb of Rangoon. At this place, eight miles north of Rangoon on the railway, where our seminary is located, on what Dr. Smith loves to call "our Newton Hill," I was privileged to spend two or three evenings with Mrs. Stevens, and from her lips to hear many incidents of the primitive days in Burma, many of them spent as were Mrs. Bennett's, associated with the Judsons in Maulmein and Rangoon. It was this dear sister to whose maternal care Edward Judson, as an infant, was entrusted when he was left motherless, and to whose care and nursing, under God, the preservation of his life was due. Very graphic were the touches given in description of the unique character of Dr. Judson — his fondness for children; his domestic tastes; his fine sense of propriety; his dauntless courage and faith. The account given of the parting scenes between Mrs. Emily C. Judson and her prostrated husband, when he was obliged to leave her for his final voyage, was very tender. Like Mrs. Bennett, Mrs. Stevens also retains the most glowing interest in the present-day work in Burma, and pleaded for its expansion with a motherly eloquence. Her transparent and spirituelle old age is something truly beautiful to look upon. Happy those who can look upon it while, like an after-glow of sunset, it lingers to warm and bless.

Dr. Cross of Toungoo has made a record of service in Burma almost as long as fifty years, and still bears abundant fruit in age. He came to the field in 1845; but we have not yet met him, and cannot speak of personal interview.

FACULTY OF THEOLOGICAL SEMINARY, INSEIN.

To meet with these honored servants of God, — the few who remain of the first generation of our workers in Burma, — and to hear from their lips experiences shared with Judson, was as if the Burman apostle himself had come back to earth for a little to remind us of the realities of his time. I count it a blessing unspeakable that my visit to Burma was, in God's providence, so timed that I could, ere they depart, catch somewhat of the spirit of these living links between the founders of the work and the present generation. Ere long the last one will have departed

CHAPTER XVI.

India.

Calcutta.

THE approach to Calcutta is a matter of dramatic interest. For many miles we pass up the Hoogly River, one of the many mouths of the Ganges. The channel is narrow, and requires skilful piloting. Many a steamer has been lost on the quicksands, that are ever shifting, and which ever stand ready to engulf any vessel which is unfortunate enough to strike them. Once aground, a vessel is certain to be swallowed up. It is a common

VIEW OF CALCUTTA.

thing to see hulks and masts projecting from the surface of the water, in the process of being completely submerged.

At intervals all along the banks, we see throngs of Hindus bathing in the sacred waters. They seem to have great camps, with multitudes of booths erected for the reception of the pilgrims. Many novel exhibitions and amusements are being carried on in connection with their superstitious festivities. Clad in pure white, they look like armies of ghosts, especially in the twilight.

Nearing the great metropolis of India, we begin to see the palaces of native princes, as well as of retired East Indian merchants, government officers, etc. Upon the picturesque palm-lined banks, as we steam up the river to our landing near old Fort William, we are impressed with the vast amount of shipping. The steamers lying at the wharves four or five abreast, with all sorts of craft for miles filling the stream, — as we have seen them at other great Eastern ports, as Yokohama, Shanghai, Hongkong, Singapore and Rangoon, — now impress us afresh that the shipping of the world is to be seen in the Eastern Hemisphere. Here all nations, except the United States, are largely represented. The morning our vessel rode into the harbor at Hongkong, we counted twenty-seven steamships of vast tonnage, representing half a score of nations. There were steamers of the French line, North German Lloyd line, half a dozen British lines, Italian, Scandinavian and Austrian lines, and *one* floating the United States flag. Arriving at Calcutta, we see similar fleets.

Europeanized India.

In the days that followed our arrival, while visiting the splendid suburbs at Barrackpore, fifteen miles above the city, and others, filled with villas of the most costly character, studding large velvety green swards, ensconced beneath great spreading banyans, — places in which the European elite of this part of India have their residences, where traders and merchant princes and queens of fashion are serving Mammon to the full, — we felt sure that the church had arrived tardily on the spot to follow up with the gospel the manifold forms of Western influence of another kind. The truth is that India, as well as other great parts of the East, has become immensely Europeanized. If you take a train from Calcutta and pass southwestward through Benares, Allahabad and Agra to Bombay, along the great railway over one of the great trunk lines, now extending for 18,000 miles through various parts of the vast

DARJEELING, IN THE HIMALAYAS.

peninsula, passing through stations of the most solid and stately character, every mile of this railway parallelled by telegraph lines, with the best of service, you will be amazed at the progress which civilization is making in this great heathen land.

These stations are manned by "babus," as they are called, — educated natives, some of them Eurasians. They manipulate the telegraph instruments, they keep the books, sell the tickets, man the capital restaurants, often conduct the trains, etc. There are 5,000,000 of these English-speaking natives in India to-day. Bombay has one of the most elaborate and costly railway stations in the world. Looking at these marks of Occidental enterprise which have filled the East, the traveller will be forced to say that whether or not missionaries go to follow up these strides of civilization with their divine work, *all the rest of the world* has made up its mind in some representative way to go East.

SERAMPORE COLLEGE.

Why should even a young lady missionary, to say nothing of men, with the Bible in her heart, who has left friends and home to go abroad, carrying the possibilities of moral renovation to great peoples, be thought a fanatic, when, upon the decks of the same steamer, say of the Peninsular and Oriental Line which she may board from London to Bombay, she will find a hundred of the most elegant ladies of English fashionable circles, promenading those decks, rustling with silks and glittering with jewels, upon the arms of army officers and merchant princes, who seem to find it no special privation, even for worldly purposes, to make their abodes in the tropics?

Our time in Calcutta was too limited for any detailed inquiries into particular features of local mission work. We visited the old Lal Bazaar Chapel, where Carey preached and Judson was baptized. We met Dr. Pentecost, and Rev. William Haslam of England, who are in the midst of special services, attended with some signs of the Lord's blessing. There seemed to be considerable stirring up on the part of European Christians, and there was evidently converting power attending the meetings held for considerable companies of Bengali young men. Many Brahmins were attracted to the meetings.

India.

Serampore.

It was an interesting morning which we were permitted to spend in visiting this early fountain head of missionary influence and power in India. We took in the old missionary college, a superb and vast edifice, containing a fine library and numerous relics suggestive of the great triumvirate who founded the institution. The original intention respecting this college was never carried out, owing to the large attention given by government to education in general, and perhaps because the Lord's blessing did not so signally attend movements largely educational. Our English brethren are still carrying on work here and training a few preachers, although the principal school work now conducted in the immense building is of a primary character.

At the side of the college is still standing the house in which Carey spent his last years. We were shown to the room in which he died. Beautiful gardens lie in the rear of the group of buildings. Passing out through the campus in front of the college building, we stood upon the historic landing ghauts on the Ganges. Up these steps Carey, Marshman and Ward passed. Boardman, Ann Hasseltine Judson and Harriet Newell also trod these sacred stones; hundreds of missionary workers have here landed, receiving welcome from those who, under God's hand, made it possible to undertake great things for God, first in India, and from thence planting themselves in regions beyond.

HOUSE IN WHICH CAREY DIED.

Up the stream a few yards, we walked under the shade of a line of immense mahogany trees which were planted by Carey's own hands. We passed the building which was originally the printing-house. We went to the cemetery, a little north of the town in a retired spot, which contains an acre of ground enclosed by a good brick wall, and found the tombs of Carey, Marshman and Ward. The tomb for Carey is a plain cenotaph, built many years ago, bearing inscriptions for himself and his wife. On one surface is inscribed "William Carey, born 17th of August, 1761, died 9th of June, 1834," and also the stanza,

> "A wretched, poor and helpless worm,
> On Thy kind arms I fall;
> Be Thou my strength and righteousness,
> My Saviour and my all."

The tombs for Marshman and Ward are also imposing and impressive, though of different form.

TOMB OF CAREY

CHAPTER XVII.

Our Assam Mission.

January 22.

ASSAM used to be, even from Calcutta, a far-distant province. When Messrs. Cutter and Brown, our first missionaries, went to Sadiya, the journey up the Brahmapootra without steam consumed five long months. Taking the mail route from Calcutta, mostly by rail, via Dhubri, and thence by steamer up the great river, we reached Gauhati in less than three days. Of course this was far short of Sadiya, which is 350 miles farther; but it was sufficient to take us into the midst of our Assam field, and was a convenient place of rendezvous for several of our missionaries to come in to meet us.

We find Assam by no means inaccessible nor out of the way in this day, even if it once was. It is a great and rich province of the Indian empire, picturesque and beautiful to the eye, especially in its upper portions, and through its twofold channels of approach, viz., the railway and the daily steamship service, within easier reach from the seaboard than Upper Burma. Three great districts of the Assam field were impressed strongly upon us from this visit; viz., the Garo district, the great plains on both sides of the river for hundreds of miles, and the Naga Hills region, various subdivisions of the numerous and accessible people of Assam.

The Garos.

These interesting people might be called the Karens of Assam. They occupy a large mountainous district in the hills south of the Brahmapootra River, and number not less than 130,000. They are a wild people, are not Hinduized, nor strictly speaking idolaters. Like the Karens, they are rather demon propitiators. They sacrifice to these spirits, sometimes even human lives, to avert dreadful calamities. So wild are these people in their mountain villages, that when our missionaries first visit them, they flee the town from fear, and hide in the forests. When won and drawn out by the gentle suasions of love, and taught, they prove manly, frank, and vigorous in all noble qualities, and far more reliable and trustworthy than the more civilized and long-perverted Hindu of the cities and plains.

MAIL CARRIER IN ASSAM.

Our two missionaries, Mason and Phillips, who have been laboring among these people for some fifteen years from their mountain centre in Tura, established by them in the very depths of the jungle, have wrought with rare skill and success, ably seconded by consecrated women.

These brethren hold annually a sort of institute for Bible study among the preachers and teachers, for some weeks preceding the association, at the place where the association is to be held for that year. This year the place was Agia, ten miles back from the river-landing, Goalpara.

On the second morning after our departure from Calcutta, Brother Gordon and I stepped ashore at Goalpara, meeting Brother Mason, who had come in with a delegation of brethren, coolies, ponies, etc., to take us out to Agia. A company of perhaps a dozen Garo Christians were waiting near our ponies upon the sands to greet us. We had gone ahead of Brother Mason, and all at once we found ourselves among this strangely expectant group. Their faces broke into sunshine as we scanned them, and in an instant we exclaimed with delight, "Oh! these are Garo Christians come to meet us!" "Yes," said Bago, one of the faithful old pastors, in half-English, as they took our luggage. We needed no introduction. Before Brother Mason could overtake us, we had shaken hands with every one of the disciples, and answered their inarticulate welcome and fellowship with our eyes and hands and hearts. "Blest be the tie that binds." We sang it together afterwards, but we experienced it even as deeply in that first glance we gave each other there on the sands at Goalpara.

In Goalpara itself, where Brother Stoddard and also Brother Keith formerly labored, we have no occupant nor even mission premises just now. Vital influences once exerted there have, however, penetrated far inland, and are far from extinct.

Taking the government road, our party was soon on the march to Agia. Through the forest road for several miles, then along a bridle-path through wild jungle-grass, across a stream or two descending from the hills, which now began to loom up at our left as we advanced, and then across well-tilled rice-fields, and past little fenced patches of mustard and sugar-cane, indicating thrift and care, we made our way to the village.

The villagers were on tip-toe of expectation. The training-class thronged at the chapel door, as we alighted. Two ruddy American missionary girls, Misses Mason and Bond, issued from the thatched and reeded mud-plastered bungalow, bidding us welcome, and announcing "tiffin" to be ready for the refreshment of our inner man. We were soon at home in Agia. We almost fancied ourselves again at the Karen Association in Burma. So pleased are these simple believers to receive us to their village. What to them was the Missionary Union was verily domiciled among them.

But what shall I say of the meeting of the day which followed? It was no gotten-up affair to show off the natives at their best. First was held a simple church meeting of the villagers to hear reports from committees on delinquents and to receive candidates for baptism, prior to the report to be made to the association. A prayer and conference meeting followed, growing out of my address to them, respecting new consecration for the evangelization of the whole Garo highlands.

So wisely have the missionaries worked in the training of this church that, under lead of its licentiate pastor, it ably conducted the whole affair. We were surprised at the parliamentary order with which each step of business was conducted; each man who had a report to make or a remark to offer, rising and addressing the moderator, giving in his word, then gathering his blanket about him again, and squatting on his mat in the most orderly way. The church clerk was, alas! a leper, but a highly worthy man. Three members, for immorality, were upon evidence excluded. Several candidates for baptism were received. The examination was more exacting and detailed by far than is common in home churches, and all open as daylight. One young woman who applied was declined after close examination, it being the conviction of some that, though they hoped she was changed, they thought she should make further proof of the fact. The pastor tenderly explained to her its significance, bade her be of good cheer, and come again at a later time. She looked sad, but the church was unanimous and firm. A youth presented himself, his father dead, his mother a heathen and opposed to his step; but he wanted to be saved, to go with the church, and he loved and trusted in Christ. He was asked if he was prepared to bear a part in church expenses. He replied that he had but little money, but he was willing to work for more. He was received, and he will surely be called on for his subscription. A middle-aged raw heathen, who had seen hard service in Satan's ways, applied, with complete confession and openness of heart. He was welcomed. And so it went on for an hour or more.

At this juncture we were introduced, and spoke to them on what the power of the gospel produces in the believer. Following the address came a prayer; then the Garo brethren opened their hearts to us, giving testimony of what the gospel had done for them.

One old man gave way to sobs, closing with a most touching prayer as he lay prone upon his face on the ground. One spoke of his "gratitude for what God has done for his people." Another said, "I am very glad to see these representatives of our society. We were lost in our sins, but the society's people have come here and helped us. We have been all these years worshipping demons, but the missionaries came and taught us, and now we are very happy." His son had been lately sick with an illness which swept the village, but God had heard prayer. His "family was as a tree that had fallen, but is now sprouted up again." Another said, "I knew I was a sinner before the missionaries came. Until I heard of Christ, I knew not where relief was to come from. Since seeing you to-day, I appreciate more than ever the love of the American Christians." A half-dozen younger men spoke in declaration of willingness to devote themselves with a whole heart to evangelizing this people.

Thus the meeting proceeded with a tenderness and pathos that assured us all that the Spirit of God was owning and attesting the utterances. Twelve years ago, when the missionaries first visited this village, the entire population ran from them like partridges to the woods. To-day there is a church here of 260 members. In a fortnight they will entertain an association with 600 delegates in attendance, representing a Garo membership of about 1,200. Are missions like these a failure?

It pays, moreover, to second such efforts as the Tura brethren are making to introduce the elements of industrial enterprise among such converts. Right thankful am I that the committee has sent out to these people an industrial missionary (likewise an ordained man) in Mr. Dring, who has lately arrived.

The Plains People.

From Agia we all went together to Gauhati for a conference. Several additional missionaries from the various stations in the upper country met us here. The Moore Brothers, together with Miss Laura Amy, a former cherished parishioner of mine in Minneapolis, just out from home, bringing to me letters and mementos of the dear ones in the family nest, journeyed from Nowgong, eighty miles, in an ox cart, to meet us. Mr. and Mrs. Clark, also from an old charge of mine in Indianapolis, came down from Molung. Mr. and Mrs. Burdette cordially entertained us all in the mission-houses formerly occupied by the Bronsons and Barkers. Mrs. Bronson also went out to Assam from the church of my first charge at Rockford, Ill.

On the Goalpara hillside a couple of days before, we had visited the spot where sleeps, in the English cemetery, Miss Marie Bronson, whom I once knew in Chicago. Two days after, while passing down the river, we met a Mrs. Harrison from Shillong, an English lady, in whose arms Miss Bronson, battling with cholera, had died in 1875, on board a river steamer.

NOWGONG MISSION-HOUSE.

How near to our hearts the *personnel* of the Assam Mission, past and present, brings us! It seems like part of our own parish, and such it is.

If on the day that we rode up from the landing to the Burdette mission-house, there had been no old and dear friends waiting on the veranda to greet us, as there were, the cordial welcome of the native church, expressed in the decorated roadway of the mission, hung with banners of welcome, with flowers and even lamps for an evening illumination, would have made us feel instantly "at home."

Much work was bestowed by the early missionaries in Assam, as Bronson, Barker, Tolman, Scott and others, upon the plains people, who dwell upon both banks of the river along the whole district from Dhubri to Sibsagor. Here dwell the Assamese proper. They are semi-Hinduized, and less susceptible to the gospel than the hills people. The apparent fruits of the valley have been rather disappointing on the whole. Much, however, must be attributed to the frequent failure in health of the laborers, or their death, and to the lamentable lack of men to take the places of the fallen. There has not been preserved such a continuity of work as to bring to large fruition the labors bestowed. As a consequence, it is not strange that native churches, often left for years together without proper oversight and instruction, should wane and almost die out. While the husbandmen have slept, the enemy has sown tares, and there have been sad defections in such churches as those at Gauhati and Nowgong, where we once had strong bases of operation. The later missionaries have had trying and painful duties in disciplining the wayward and purging out the leaven of evil. These same brethren, however, have had encouragements in their work, particularly as they have worked outward in surrounding villages.

Among these millions of people who throng the lowlands, there are no representatives of the gospel except ourselves; and there can be no question but a real and continuous and forceful occupancy of the river towns and adjacent districts would in the end prove very fruitful. We cannot without great infidelity abandon the work undertaken. Besides, if we should give up the plains, we cut away our base of supplies for the highly promising work of the hills, and invite Romanists and ritualists to come and build on the old foundations we have painfully laid.

The Nagas.

Our interview with Mr. and Mrs. Clark, who came down from Molung to meet us, opened up to us the various peoples of the Naga race, and the fine promise which these people, bordering on the northwest of Burma, afford to gospel effort. Among these hill peoples, doubtless also allied to the Karens, we count four great tribes of Nagas, the Mishmis and Singphos, all allied to the Kachins. These peoples are all accessible, and they have repeatedly sent delegations to our missionaries requesting teachers. If the Union were able to send several new families to enter in among these hopeful, hungering people, there can be no doubt that a work, in every element the counterpart of our Burman work among the Karens, could soon be developed. We are entering in among the Kachins, assisted by the Karens from Bhamo. Could we now also begin work from these adjacent tribes behind the Kachins, working back from the Brahmapootra on the one side, and from the Irrawaddy on the other, we might fairly join the work in Assam and Burma, thus strengthening both.

A Meeting with the Brahmo Somaj.

January 23.

Last night we had a most interesting meeting with a society of the Brahmo Somaj, the Unitarians of India. Observing a fine little chapel on one side of the town with a pleasant garden, we ventured in just at sunset, and found a half-dozen bright and intelligent Hindus. They seemed inclined to converse, and pleased that we called in. They explained that it was their anniversary day; that they were to have a meeting an hour later, and invited us to attend, though the exercises would be in Bengali. These, however, spoke English.

After dinner we returned. It was a queer service. They played much on Hindu instruments, chanting a weird sort of psalm or sentimental ode on "Wake, O Sluggish Mind," etc.; then for a half-hour they prayed, one after another, to the "One Spiritual God," in whom they professed to believe.

MISSION CHAPEL, SIBSAGOR.

When we went away, a half-dozen of them followed us, evidently desiring to know what we thought of the service, and thanked us for attending. I then addressed them as tenderly as I knew how, for I had hoped to get a chance to preach to them. I commended them for abandoning idolatry, but urged that they needed to come further — to Christ, in fact, and to the Bible. One of them desired to argue. Him I avoided; another one seemed hungry for the truth. I pressed on him and on the others the experimental method in testing Christianity. One seemed much moved. When I had preached my little sermon on how they might know Christ, I prayed for them, kneeling in the street, pleading earnestly for them then and there. It was a new experience, there in the moonlight on the banks of the Brahmapootra. I gave my testimony, at least, which I hope will not be lost.

One of them followed me home, and we talked till near midnight. I got him down on his knees, and it was touching to hear him beg for forgiveness for his great sins, and that God would not let him die unpardoned; but like any American sinner, he shrank from accepting Christ's atonement. This man was the high-school teacher; decidedly well informed respecting even the Bible and Christ. He said as we parted, "You have at least done your part kindly for me, and your skirts are clear." He was an Assamese. He asked for a missionary to be sent to Dhubri. I replied, "My dear fellow, with all the light that you have respecting the true God and the Bible, you yourself ought to become the missionary; and what is more, God will hold you responsible if you do not."

From Calcutta to Bombay.

We left Calcutta for Bombay by rail, making two or three stops at places full of historic interest. The first was at Benares, the great headquarters of Hinduism. We shall never forget the melancholy awe with which we moved up and down the river on the boat, taking in the miles of massive ruins of Mohammedan and Hindu architecture, which are half-buried in confusion, on lofty terraces for hundreds of feet high overlooking the majestic river. The thousands of bathers in the sacred waters; the poor mourners who stood wailing upon the terraces, looking down upon the funeral pyres, where the bodies of their dead were being reduced to ashes, were something sad beyond description. The sombre figures of the various fakirs, sitting in ashes amid some old ruin, leaning upon a staff, or hanging by ropes to support bodies which were said not to have sat for sixty years, with long masses of hair, matted with mud and filth, streaming down their shoulders, looking out of eyes that were strange and inhuman, made a scene of tragic impressiveness. The filth and uncleanness were unspeakable. We were glad to get away from the horrors of the place. The "Light of Asia" is said to have emanated from near this spot. Indeed, five miles out from Benares, we visited some old ruins of a monastery where Siddhartha Gautama is said to have begun his preaching. The whole region is a sorry comment on anything professing to have light in it. It is the best sample of the blackness of darkness in the earthly condition of a people which my eyes have ever looked upon.

We spent a day at Cawnpore, where are the memorials of the Sepoy Rebellion, and heard from those who were eye witnesses of those distressing times details of the cruelties of Indian

WORSHIP OF GANESHA, BENARES.

TAJ MIHAL

treachery and the sufferings of innocent women and children, who were slaughtered by hundreds, and some buried alive.

We went to Agra and saw the picturesque fort, the Pearl Mosque, and the many symbols of mogul dynasties now gone forever. Of course we saw the Taj Mahal, the most peerless tomb in the world, a dream of loveliness, a poem in marble. It has been described a hundred times — it has never been described; it can only be felt. By moonlight especially, it is like a house not made with hands. Of all expressions of human love that ever embodied itself in architecture, this is supreme. From Agra we came on to Bombay, a long, hot ride.

Bombay.

Calcutta, Madras, Bombay! These are the three great commercial cities of India. In many respects Bombay is the most impressive of the three. It contains extraordinary specimens of classic English architecture — such buildings as the High Court, the Cathedral, the Cathedral school, the various government buildings, hotels, railway stations, colleges, etc.

What Glasgow is to Great Britain, that Bombay is to India — a great port, a vast merchandizing emporium, a solidly built, modernized, tumultuous city. Traders, merchantmen and all sorts of skilful artificers are here — Hindu, Mohammedan, Parsee, Arab, Kashmir, African and European. It has the rush of Chicago, the fashion of Paris, and the cosmopolitanism of London. Passing through great portions of it, you would scarcely think yourself to be in Asia. It is half occidental, half oriental. The crescent-shaped bay on which it stands, embossed with islands, with here and there rocky coasts, lends a Neapolitan beauty to the situation.

A drive around the beach on the chief boulevard at sunset gives you a view of the world's fashion altogether unique, because it is so composite. What varieties of headgear and costume and vehicle, in colors as manifold as those of the dying dolphin! Apart from the vigorous work here prosecuted by the Salvation Army under Mr. Ballington Booth, we saw but little of mission work. Bombay has extensive and successful missions, but limits of time forbade our exploration.

The Parsees, or fire-worshippers, are numerous in Bombay. In externals they impressed us as an attractive people; intelligent, keen-eyed, genteel, philosophic, even poetical. We visited their strange depository for the dead, — the far-famed "Towers of Silence," as they are called. These are simply great cylindrical towers of stone masonry, standing in a high, rocky garden of surpassing beauty in the outskirts of the city. In these towers the Parsees place their dead, exposed without coffins, and within a couple of hours all the flesh is picked from the bones of the dead by flocks of vultures kept for the purpose. The sun then bleaches the bones to decomposition. Such are the notions of a people who, knowing not "Jesus and the resurrection," have fallen into this strange treatment of their dead.

CHAPTER XVIII.

On the Telugu Field.

The Deccan.

WE approached this field by rail from the Bombay side. From Calcutta around to Madras is a long and tedious journey, consuming, if unbroken, four days and nights. At Wadi, about two thirds of the way from Bombay to Madras, we were met by several of our missionaries in " the Deccan," so called, or the Nizam's dominions; and there we were detained for a day of conference respecting the work in this particular district. In certain respects this field is distinct from the old original Telugu field. Here in the centre of India is a native independent empire, under the rule of the Nizam, with Hyderabad for its capital. It is the strongest Mohammedan centre in India. Nevertheless, in the midst of this dominion our workers, pioneered by Brother Campbell, who is now resting in America, have effected a vigorous entrance, and great blessing has attended the work.

We have established stations at Secunderabad, Palmur, Hanamaconda and Nalgonda, in all of which fruit from among the Telugu people has been gathered. The missionaries working here are Brother Maplesden and wife, at Secunderabad; Brother Chute, wife and sister, at Palmur, and Brother Friesen and wife, at Nalgonda.

NIZAM'S PALACE, HYDERABAD.

The station at Hanamaconda, where we have a good mission-house and a chapel, has been unoccupied for two years.

Our conference was held in a railway car which was placed at our disposal, and served for a chapel by day and a lodging-place at night. To hear those earnest brethren and sisters represent, not only the needs, but also the rare promise of this great district, in which they so eagerly toil, was enough to melt adamant. To them the work is a living joy, and they wonder that other helpers do not come to share in toil so exalted and so rewarding. Not all fields by any means are so ripe as this.

DECCAN MISSIONARIES, SECUNDERABAD.

The Deccan missionaries represent that the tidings of good things and the inspiration arising from the work in the older district about Ongole, have communicated themselves to the region where they are laboring. The wave of blessing seems to sweep northwestward, and workers only are needed to soon gather thousands of believers into the kingdom.

Other denominations not only wonder that we are so slow to follow up such an advantage, but also think us on some fields so criminally negligent, — as, for example, at Hanamaconda, — that they regard our primacy there as about forfeited. They will desist from entering such fields no longer, but will proceed to reap the harvest which we are likely to allow to fall back into the ground.

A EURASIAN GIRL.

We met on this field Bishop Thoburn, than whom no man in India is more zealous or influential. He seems to know how to obtain both men and money to continually enlarge his work. His efficient superintendence of Methodist interests is phenomenal.

Work for Eurasians.

My detention at Wadi and the limits of my time prevented me from going to Madras. Mr. W. went, however, greeting the brethren who awaited our coming, and preaching for them on the Sabbath. He also brought away some fine photographs of the valuable mission property lately offered to our board by the English Baptists. The general feeling is that this action will prove a wise thing for them, and in every way advantageous to our work, especially in the matter of raising up from among the East Indians or Eurasians, workers and assistants for our missionaries.

What I have observed on all hands in India has impressed me with the immense importance of utilizing this Eurasian element among the Indian people for our own sakes, if we would manifold our local hold on communities, and for their sakes also, and for the sake of the native populations whose language they speak, and to whom they are our best interpreters. These Eurasians are readily Christianized. They are permanently identified with Indian life and well-being, fully acclimated, and habituated to life among Asiatics. They are a valuable go-between, as touching both Eastern and Western nations. Besides, more than likely, this is providentially their divine mission. Bishop Thoburn is giving primary and chief attention to these people as an ultimate means of reaching the heathen. The Methodists are both evangelizing and educating the Eurasians.

JULIA.

Conference at Nellore.

From Wadi we proceeded directly to Nellore, where it was arranged that a conference of all the coast missionaries should assemble. Nearly all were present, a score or more, and for two days we had delightful intercourse. Veterans in the work, — as Clough, Downie and Boggs, — returned workers, — as Drake, Manley and Thomssen, — several sisters, and new recruits, — as Hadley, Heinrichs and others, — were there. Records of past achievements and anticipations for the future were dwelt upon.

Great concern filled the minds of all as to how existing and prospective vacancies are to be filled. Brethren fainting from long strain, and compelled soon to go home for recuperation, with the added pain of leaving their stations to vacancy or to eager proselyters, constrained our deepest sympathy.

The native church which assembled to greet us, and hear our message, filled us with great interest. Preachers, students and Bible-women, trophies of Christ's gospel, won our hearts. Characters like old Lydia, and Julia, — that modern prophetess, — and her husband, Kanakiah, filled us with thankful wonder. The industrial school, under Dr. Downie's fostering care, commanded our admiration. The seasons of united prayer we had together, were perhaps the most blest hours of all.

Ramapatam.

From Nellore we proceeded, in company with Dr. and Mrs. Boggs and Miss Dr. Cummings, to Ramapatam. That was a unique ride, in a veritable *pull-man* car. In Dr. Downie's rockaway wagon we were wheeled by eight coolies over the forty-five miles in about ten hours. We changed coolies every ten miles.

Our stay at Ramapatam was brief but pleasing. We found the seminary a real beehive of activity. A choicer, sweeter-spirited man than Dr. Boggs we could not have at the head of that

BROWNSON SEMINARY, RAMAPATAM.

school. Now, after being long overworked, he is happily reinforced by his son. The native teachers impressed us as choice men. We looked with satisfaction into the kind of teaching, biblical and other, that is being done. We addressed the 125 students assembled in the chapel of Brownson Hall on "Truth Experienced the Preacher's Power." It was all through an inter-

156   *In Brightest Asia.*

preter, of course; but never had we more eager hearing nor more sympathetic response. Evidently these men "know" God and "the things which are freely given unto us of God." The after-speeches of the teachers "Daniel," "John" and "Samuel" gave us added assurance of soundness, both of head and heart, as well as their real apprehension of the message we brought to them.

Ongole.

Another ride, partly by night in our coolie carriage, and we drew up in the early morning before the mission-house of Dr. Clough, at Ongole. The missionary met us at the door with a lantern, and ushered us to our chamber for a little rest.

ONGOLE HIGH SCHOOL.

In the morning we were soon ready for the round of the half-dozen or more schools of which the mission is so justly proud. The various "palam" or hamlet primaries; the intermediates; the wondrously engaging caste-girls' schools, filled with the petite bejewelled little ladies from high-rank families of the town; and above all the high school — to our surprise quite a college — were visited one by one.

We were not, however, prepared for such receptions as we had; for wreaths of marigold to be hung about our necks by the children; for spray baths of rose water showered over us; and for other earnests of Indian welcome. The kindergarten work, the lovely plays of the caste girls, would have delighted Froebel himself.

At the high school, with its enthusiastic head master and its 200 boys, a prepared address was read and presented to us. When we began to respond, and turned about for our interpreter, we were told that we would be understood quite well in English. This was a wonder. We proceeded for twenty minutes, and point after point was responded to with cheers. This gave us a new token, not only that the Anglo-Saxon tongue is conquering all other tongues, but also that the East Indian student is as fully alive as his Western brothers. These boys and hosts of others, including Brahmin gentlemen of the town, petition that this school be made a college. Can we prevent it? Dare we turn these inquisitive, alert youths of India over to non-Christian schools? Here is a question for the wisdom of the wisest, and may the Most High help us!

DR. J. E. CLOUGH.

Interview with Brahmins.

During our visit to Ongole, we were one evening interviewed by a company of about a dozen Hindu gentlemen of the town, including several Brahmins and others of high-caste distinction. Some of these men were high officials of government, one of them being a district munsiff, or judge, another a sub-registrar, etc. Their object in obtaining the interview was threefold; viz., to express their welcome to an official of the American Baptist Missionary Union; to commend to him, in the strongest terms, the work wrought by our devoted missionaries in their land, and to petition that the valuable educational work instituted by our mission be further prosecuted, and that especially the high school at Ongole be raised to the status of a second-grade college.

A movement had been instituted in the town, on the part of certain of the straitest sect of the Hindus, to maintain a sort of rival school, conducted on Hindu principles and at private expense. In the meeting above referred to, this whole matter was discussed in the presence of Dr. Clough and other missionaries. All united in the strongest commendation of our mission school work. The

MR. RUNGANADAM PILLAI.

strictest Hindus even, in the event of maintaining their own school in the town, avowed the desire that it should be a feeder to our high school, especially if it should be made a college.*

One of these gentlemen, Mr. Runganadam Pillai, was opposed to the Hindu school altogether, and in terms of great boldness and rare eloquence pleaded for concentration on the mission high school. In the course of his argument, he urged that the work of the mission school, under the control of the missionaries, is the only force which goes to the root of the evils which inhere in Hinduized society. "Leave the work of education entirely in the hands of Dr. Clough, who has done so much for a town like Ongole, and who has thrown his heart and soul together for educating our children and for our well being."

The address, delivered in excellent English, came with such hot fervency, with such bold energy, in the very face of his Brahmin brethren, and with such surprise withal, that I afterwards requested the gentleman to write out his address for me. This he did, and sent it by the hand of Dr. Clough, remarking in the note which accompanied the speech, "There is some readable matter here which our American brethren must see."

Religious Degeneration in India.

Referring to the address of one of his Brahmin friends, which had preceded his, in which claim was made that the ancient Aryan ancestors of the Brahmins worshipped also one true God as the missionaries do, Mr. Runganadam proceeded to trace the historical degeneration of the Indian peoples from the early Aryan times, period by period through the Vedic period, the Puranic, through the periods when Kapila and Buddha, with their agnostic theories arose, through the period when the worship of idols, fetichism, and the caste system came in. His summation ran thus:—

"In the first age, the Hindu mind recognized God and the equality of men; in the second, it doubted God, and introduced the caste system; in the third, it denied the government of God, and admitted the equality of men; in the fourth, it firmly established idol-worship and caste distinctions. Thus stage by stage, the great fundamental doctrines of the fatherhood of God and the brotherhood of man were stamped out from our minds. The pernicious caste system surrounds us on all sides from the day of our birth to the day of our death. It has bound our hand and foot together. We are under its yoke, and are now the willing slaves of this monster tyrant and intolerant taskmaster. It has sown the seeds of disunion and discord among us, made all honest manual labor contemptible in our sight, shut out all internal and external commerce, brought on physical degeneracy, and destroyed the germs of individuality and independence of character."

"It has first enslaved us by the most abject spiritual tyranny, and then prepared us to take the yoke of foreign slavery. It has made the various classes of people to look upon each other with contempt. They appear more as enemies than as friends in their social relations.

"The condition of women among us is wretched in the extreme. An infant girl is married at ten, and at twelve or thirteen often becomes a mother — most revolting, indeed, to the sense

---

* This Hindu school has since been abandoned.

of a rational being—and the child mother often becomes a grandmother at the age of thirty. Children born of such parents are extremely weak and puny creatures, often crawling on all fours, and soon find an early grave. If they live, they prove effeminate, feeble in body and mind. If an infant girl loses her husband, she becomes a widow, and is doomed to be a moving grave throughout her whole existence, because our cruel customs cannot allow her to re-marry."

Indian Reforms Futile.

"We are considering reforms. Some think that reform must proceed from within, while others hold that it must come from without. But show me one instance where we ourselves, unaided by the missionaries, have produced such changes as I plead for, in the amelioration of the condition of the masses, who are the backbone of the country. The Indian reformer merely, struggles hard and in vain. He has not yet succeeded in his attempts to any appreciable degree. He is, rather, baffled on all sides.

I do not think I would wound the feeling of my friends here (Brahmins) if I say we cannot, unaided, accomplish the results needed. We may honestly endeavor, but the very structure of our social fabric does not permit us to succeed. The work must be placed in the hands of more earnest and able men than ourselves. We have not the force of character nor the moral courage to do what is needed for the common good, for the improvement of a common society. Times, however, are changing, and we see the signs of life reviving. We must, therefore, try to acquire those virtues which we are said to lack, and to free ourselves from the faults with which we are justly charged. These lessons we must still learn, I think, from our English and American brethren; and till we learn them we must put our children under their care and management."

"For these reasons, I think there is no necessity for another high school to rival the mission school, and the work may be handed over to Dr. Clough, who will continue to do as he does now, impart both secular and spiritual education to our children with all parental care, and teach them also a sense of duty and strength for duty."

Testimony to Missionaries.

"Who are these missionaries, and what have they already done for us? When as a people, as the result of the deteriorating process I described a few moments ago, we were fast sinking beneath the weight of ignorance and of the priestly and Mohammedan tyranny, England came to the rescue, like a godsend to give her helping hand. The Englishman, indeed, came here at first as a mere merchant. He made money, and went back to his native country to enrich it. He came again as often as he liked. finally fought for our country, and won it.

DR. LYMAN JEWETT.

"But in the case of a missionary who came in the wake of his brother merchant, what do we find? Did he come to make money, hoard it up, and take it back to the land of his birth, like the merchant? Had he any permanent interest in the land of his sojourn? He had neither the one nor the other. He was separated from his kith and kin, and sailed from the land of freedom to the land of slaves. He had neither relative nor friend in this strange land, except his Bible in his pocket. He planted a small church in a foreign land, preached the gospel to an alien nation, and was subject to the laws of Oriental government. He worked under many disadvantages, identified himself with strange people, and never saw his lovely home or the sweet faces of his family or friends left behind. He often got the tropical fever without any-

TELUGU MISSIONARIES.

body to attend upon him. He was weary and tired; had at times nothing to eat, and did not know where to lay his head in the evening after a hard day of labor. He became the friend of the poor, and the poor received him kindly. He was often beaten, stoned, annoyed or insulted in the course of his work, but he meekly bore all these hardships because he knew that 'the blood of the martyrs is the seed of the church.'

"Why did he thus toil in a tropical clime, and die at last in a strange land 'unwept, unhonored, and unsung'? Reasons for such self-sacrifice are not far to seek. Was it not for the sake of humanity? for the sake of truth? He saw face to face the deplorable condition of the people without a God and without a common society, and he therefore made himself a self-sacrifice to the righteous cause."

"Instances of such missionary devotion are not wanting in our country. Turn and see where Schwartz, Flaxman, Carey and St. Francis Xavier, and a host of others lie buried. They were the pioneers of our new civilization, before government schools and colleges were opened. It is this small band of devout missionaries that have implanted the fair tree of freedom in our soil, nourished it, fostered it with all tender care, and brought it to its present condition. It is not yet in full bearing. It is they that have diffused education, and made the gentle stream of Western civilization and culture flow at our very doors."

The Uplifting of Outcasts.

"The missionary has already done much, and the remarkable thing is that his best achievements have been wrought among that class of people whom we have been taught most to despise. These are the pariahs of society,— either agriculturists or agricultural laborers,— the low-caste man in India, physically strong, but morally coward, because so long subject to social and spiritual tyranny and degeneracy.

"It is from this low-caste people that the present Christian population of Ongole is mainly recruited. It musters strong here; it is increasing by rapid strides, and it is likely to submerge beneath it the other classes at no distant day, if these Christian masses are only educated. The Christians are now taught to read and write, though this had been denied to them before, and to learn the sense of duty and a strength for duty. Their posterity is also increasing proportionately as they themselves are on the increase.

"In connection with this movement, we may now see in the same mission school and in the same class-room the boys of the low caste and the no caste sitting side by side on the same bench with the caste Hindu boys. They touch each other, and exchange views, thoughts and sentiments with each other, and there grows up a mutual respect. Is not this a great change, and does it not promise a bright future for our sons? Is not this an honest and successful endeavor to bring together various broken-up societies, and agglutinate them into one homogeneous mass?

"To complete this success, we must unite with the kind missionary who stands as a medium between the higher and lower classes of people. Moreover, the sort of education afforded by the mission school, especially if they shall go on to exalt its grade, will render more skilful the mission's catechists and preachers, enable them better to understand the nobler truths in the Bible, and to meet the arguments of the educated Hindus who yet resist."

At the close of the evening on which the above address, with several others, was given, these same Brahmin gentlemen invited me to preach to them on the following evening (Sunday). This I did, and was listened to with an attention and enthusiasm that surprised me. Moreover, these very gentlemen sat serenely amid low-caste peoples and others of the town who came in to give me audience, as if they had no thought of caste scruples.

On the Monday morning before I left, two of these same Brahmins came to see me privately, showing evidence of real conviction for sin. Not only did they permit me to pray for them, but they each prayed for themselves in the name of Jesus Christ.

162   *In Brightest Asia.*

[Later, when Dr. Clough came to leave India to come to America, these high-caste gentlemen of Ongole gathered to a farewell meeting given in his honor; and among other things said by them in their addresses was this, spoken by Mr. Dhara Markundayula Sastry (a Brahmin and private banker): "According to the Shastras, I should not have stirred out of my house to-day, as there was a ceremony to be performed by me this day; but whatever the Shastras may require, they could not prevent my being present to do honor to Dr. Clough, who has done so much for our people and country."

On this occasion a prepared address, engrossed on parchment, was read to the missionary, and afterwards was sent to him in this country, encased in an elegant silver casket.]

BAPTISTERY AT ONGOLE.

The Sabbath at Ongole was a high day. The chapel was thronged at 9 o'clock in the morning with 666 Sunday-school scholars. Eighteen hundred texts of Scripture were recited. It was as orderly as Deacon Chipman's old school at Tremont Temple, or as Brother Jacobs' in Chicago. At 11 o'clock Dr. Clough preached to the throngs which now filled all the outside verandas, as well as the chapel. At 2 o'clock candidates presented themselves for baptism, and ninety-seven were received. These Brother W. and I baptized, just before sunset, in that historic pool under the tamarind tree in Dr. Clough's garden, where not less than 10,000 souls have been buried and raised again with their Lord. The "Lone Star" has become a galaxy. It was an exalted privilege to have a little part in this renowned and apostolic work.

Off to Camp at Chendalur.

On Monday we started, in company with Dr. Clough, in his famous covered ox cart, for a tour through a few of the 450 villages in which the Ongole disciples dwell, and to pitch camp for a couple of days at Chendalur, fifty miles across the country towards Cumbum, the last station we could visit on the Telugu field. On we went, all Monday afternoon and through the whole night.

Every few miles we would fetch up at a village, and from a score to a hundred of the Christians would assemble, sing a hymn for us, ask for a prayer, and then, amid a chorus of "*Salaams*,"

CAMP AT CHENDALUR.

they would seize our cart, and draw us on a mile or so, and thus "send us on our way after a godly sort."

Through all hours of the night they waited for us, and with lanterns and torches came to greet us. Some came from new villages, begging for a teacher and for the word of God, and they would not take "No" for an answer. Some came clasping our knees, and all but worshipping us in thanks for the gifts of missionaries and the gospel. But after we had reached camp the next day, what scenes awaited us!

That Tuesday was a high day in our lives. Probably 2,000 people came in to see us. It was a great camp meeting. You should have seen them bring presents to me, — chickens, eggs, parcels of sugar; and two live rams were sent from two village chiefs.

Native preachers, with numbers of candidates for baptism, were already gathered, and through all the day they kept coming in companies of from six to thirty. By noon there were groups on all sides being catechised and examined. Idolatry and the badges of Hinduism were renounced and surrendered; notably the lock of hair sacred to Vishnu was in numerous cases shorn off. Preaching services were held. An audience of hundreds sat or stood about us while Dr. Clough, the native preachers and ourselves discoursed to them.

Baptizing Experiences.

At 5 o'clock in the afternoon the baptisms began. Five hundred candidates had been received. What a scene it was! Like a repetition of the occasion when of old the multitudes went out unto John at the Jordan. We baptized till dark, and, wearied, bade others wait till morning. Many slept under the trees, and next morning 150 more came and were received; and even at noon, when we were obliged to break camp to reach our train ten miles away, we left ninety-seven others waiting for the ordinance; and as we journeyed along the road, groups of yet others, by sixes and by tens, were coming. These were despatched to Dr. Clough's camp, twenty miles away, for the morrow, when their cases would be heard.*

The truth is, that the whole region has been practically won to confidence in the missionary who for twenty-five consecutive years, with wondrous tact and zeal, has devoted his whole being to this people. On the twenty-eighth day of last December, 1,671 were baptized at Ongole. Not less than 3,500 will be gathered in this year on the Ongole field alone. But oh, what a dearth of teachers for those 450 villages in which the converts reside! Poor they are beyond conception, but they know Christ and the missionary. It was pitiful to hear them " beg for teachers," to be " taught to read," etc. I shall not soon forget the case of one man, who followed us for a mile or two, holding on to the side of our ox cart, trotting after us as we rapidly drove across the plain to a distant station. He was a man of fine physique and noble, regular features, with nicely trimmed hair and a clear, piercing eye. As he earnestly chatted away with Dr. Clough, I asked what he was talking about. "Oh," said the Doctor, "he wants to come to Ongole to learn to read." "What?" said I, "can't that man read? Look at his fine features, his manly self-poise." "No," said the Doctor. Said I, "Ask him why he wishes to learn to read." The question was put. "That I may read the Bible," was the reply. "Ask him why he wants to read the Bible," I further queried. Dr. Clough repeated my question to him. With a look which will be with me till my dying day, the noble fellow looked up; his eyes met mine as he earnestly answered, "*I want food for my heart!*" Said I to Dr. Clough, " Let him come to your school, if he is forty years of age and has a family; don't turn any man away who ' wants food for his heart.'" Dr. Clough told him what I said, and invited him to come up to the next quarterly meeting at Ongole. "*Salaam*," said the delighted man, and away he went across the

---

* In fact, within the next week after Dr. Clough parted from us, he baptized 600 more. In one case the whole village accepted Christianity, pulling down their idol-house, and giving up to the missionary their idols, some of which he afterwards brought to us.

plain to his home, to make arrangements to get ready for the anticipated period of study at the mission capital.

Will the American Baptists tell us how these evangelized multitudes are to be trained and built up into a compact spiritual house, unless missionaries on this field, pressed to breaking in this colossal work, are mightily and speedily reinforced?

The Cumbum Pentecost.

November 11.

From Chendalur we went to Donakonda, and, bidding Dr. Clough farewell, took the train for Cumbum. We supposed the enthusiastic welcome accorded us had reached its climax on the Ongole field; but no. I fear, indeed, that "I should become a fool in glorying" if I should tell of all that awaited us as we arrived on the Cumbum district. At three successive stations on the railway, companies of the native Christians of a couple of hundred each, hearing of our approach, had come out to meet us with their excited "*Salaams*" and with little presents, as they stood drawn up alongside of our train for recognition.

The people on the train did not know what to make of it. They had scarcely seen anybody receive such wholesale honor from these poor non-caste people. The viceroy of India would have scarcely had a more eager welcome.

Arrived at Cumbum, where we could only spend the night, the darkness had come on, and we were deploring that we should be unable to see the compound by daylight. But our fears had been anticipated. As we rode into the yard fronting the mission-house, drawn in an American buggy with ten fleet students of the school for steeds, suddenly "*Salaams*" from 600 throats saluted our ears. The flame of a huge bonfire illumined the place. School children raised a song of welcome. Banners with finely lettered greetings, such as "Welcome" and "God bless our secretary," and the like over-arched the way.

The veteran preacher "Abraham" seized my hand with both of his, and like another Simeon broke forth, "Lord, now lettest thou thy servant depart in peace."* He afterwards begged the privilege of walking all the way down to the railway station, and bearing a lantern to light the way for us, a distance of four miles, at the hour of midnight, to which, of course, we did not consent. At the meeting in the chapel, he prayed for us like a prophet, thanking God "that the shepherd is among us," and praising God for the "reception of such a gospel, even that of the covenant through the precious blood of Christ, which our American brethren have sent us."

There was one man in Mrs. Newcomb's house, a converted caste man, formerly a priest, who I verily believe would have worshipped me, if I had not stopped him. He bowed his face on my hands repeatedly, held his hands on my head with such devotion, and embraced me till I was unable to endure it. I despair of describing the reception given us at the Newcomb compound.

The eager youths of the school sent up sky-rockets, and kindled throughout the twenty-acre compound bonfires, which so illumined the whole place that we saw everything as if by daylight. The girls' school; the fine oriental well, worthy to be compared with Hezekiah's Pool in Jerusalem; the rising new mission-house, so long needed; the stately grove of tamarind trees;

* This old man has since passed away peacefully to his reward.

the spacious chapel, and the handsome baptistery were all visible and redolent under the illumination.

Here again we found waiting for baptism forty-four recent converts from the Weaver caste, the first-fruits of a coming harvest from the higher ranks. Being personally too weary myself, Brother W. again stood me in stead in administering the ordinance. A quiet, impressive and inspiring scene it all made.

Then came the meeting in the chapel, with addresses, singing, responses, prayers, etc. Probably 700 persons were present. We were obliged to take the train for Bombay the next morning; and as the railway was four miles away, we preferred to go to the station to sleep a little, leaving at 11 o'clock. So all this had to be packed into one evening. We had such a time shaking the people off when we came to leave. We were captives of a gratitude that was touching in the extreme. Well, all this was hardly foreseen when I baptized those two people (Mr. and Mrs. Newcomb) in Indianapolis ten years ago. "What hath God wrought!"

After making all due allowance for the glow of this reception, due in part to the gladness of our missionaries, Mr. and Mrs. Newcomb, to receive a former pastor who had baptized them, we can calmly say that the Cumbum Christians have the true ring. The great meeting in the chapel which followed the baptism gave opportunity for them, in addresses, prayers and songs, to give proof of their genuine quality. Great blessing has attended Brother Newcomb's work from the first. In the year just closing, he has been permitted to record 1,200 baptisms, and 200 more are entered on the new year. He was lately petitioned to visit one district in which it is said 600 are waiting for the ordinance.* He seems to have his native assistants well in hand. Mrs. Newcomb's work in the school is also most effective.

Had we had time to visit other stations like Bapatla, Nursaravapetta and others, we should have seen similar things. The work of ingathering is by no means confined to the Ongole and Cumbum districts. At Palmur, Vinukonda and Nalgonda, numbers of converts are also coming in, and no part of the Telugu field is without fruitage.

An Impending Crisis.

Such were some of the many heart-filling experiences which we were graciously permitted to enjoy in our brief visit to this mission. Many good things, less demonstrative, but quite as genuine and full of promise, must remain untold. Many dark, dark scenes are there. The very greatness of this ingathering precipitates a crisis. The converts, as a rule, are untutored, poor almost to beggary, and in need of even the most primary instruction and discipline in the whole round of living. Our force is entirely inadequate to begin to do this properly. Unless we do have speedy and large re-enforcements, there is grave danger that in the near future, when some of the veterans shall have fallen and the personal magnetism, which has so long and well held them to us is departed, we shall have disastrous fallings away to face. May God prevent such a calamity!

* In fact, he found many times that number, who have since been gathered in, in numbers so large as to be startling, — about 3,000 of them.

CHAPTER XIX.

In Bible Lands.

Arabian Sea.

Steamship " Peninsular," February 15.

ONE day out from Bombay, headed for home, having completed most happily my peregrinations on the six mission-fields of Japan, China, Malaysia, Burma, Assam and India; all this without a day's illness or the least touch of fever of any kind, and amid scenes which, beyond any others of a previous lifetime, have been gratifying to my inmost heart. Surely I should be a thankful soul to-day, as I know you will be, when you read the lines announcing the completion of this record. My gratitude to our preserving God is further heightened by the reflection that in all these six months of our separation, my dear family flock have also been spared from accident or illness, which would at least have interfered with the serenity of mind, so desirable to one who is called upon to take in so much as I have been expected to. I have been highly favored also, in being able to see so many of the very persons I most wished to meet on these fields.

Yesterday at 2 P.M. we set sail in this superb ship, with some hundreds of pleasant passengers, including the Bishop of Lahore, Sir Charles Crossthwaite, late chief commissioner of Burma, a couple of lords and barons, etc. Mr. Armstrong of Maulmein, Miss Tschirch of Bassein, Miss Bunn of Prome, Mrs. Cochrane of Toungoo, and we two Baptist bishops composed the missionary party. As usual, we have perfection of weather, smooth seas, and we glide on towards Aden, our first landing-place, as serenely as possible.

Aden.

February 23.

Aden we found a strange, desolate, Mohammedan sort of a place. The rocks, which tower, rugged and bare, on every hand, are Gibraltar-like in grandeur, and fortified by

SUEZ CANAL.

the English to the highest pitch. We went ashore, and drove from the landing about five miles away to the city, where we saw, amid the fastnesses of the rocks, ancient pools, said to have been prepared by Solomon. The whole district was alive with camels, Arabs having ostrich plumes to sell, and gamins crying "backsheesh!"

Red Sea and Mt. Sinai.

Yesterday was the Sabbath, spent on the Red Sea. In the afternoon I preached on the "Event of the Crossing." (Heb. xi. 29.) It was an elevating experience, dwelling, as I did, upon the crises of life which the ancient physical miracle symbolized. There were no dull listeners. How could there be, in such a place, with Mt. Sinai itself almost in sight, — really so in the early morning following?

Alexandria.

Khedive Steamship "Mahalla," ALEXANDRIA HARBOR, February 26.

We are just off for Jaffa, reversing the order, I hope, of a certain prophet of old who vainly trusted to reach Tarshish. We came from Cairo last night by train. We had only this morning until 10 o'clock to see Alexandria, but in reality there is very little to see, as compared with Cairo.

The only ancient relic of consequence is Pompey's Pillar, a lofty granite shaft, terminating in a Corinthian capital. Its date is the fourth century, A.D., and was probably in honor of the Roman emperor, Diocletian, as the books say. The site of the old Pharos, or lighthouse, is pointed out, while a new modern affair stands farther out on the point or horn of artificial reef which encloses the harbor.

The site of the city is on low, flat, uninteresting ground. On the limestone coast to the southward, stand a lot of quaint old windmills, suggestive of Holland; while a little above the water line and under where the windmills stand, can be seen rows of entrances to ancient catacombs.

In driving about the city, one is struck with the half-Grecian character of people, costumes, etc. Many of the shop signs are written in Greek characters. The characteristics of the people, however, are a mighty deterioration on the old model we cherish in sentiment. Of course the Turkish and Egyptian characters prevail. Traces of the Arabic and Mohammedan are much less marked than in Cairo. Even the donkey boys are scarce, as compared with Cairo.

THE SHIP OF THE DESERT.

Cairo.

All day yesterday we gave to Cairo, which is modern Egypt. We visited the Citadel, the mosques, the great Mohammedan College of El Azhar, with its 10,000 students, besides driving through wonderfully antique and curious streets; peered into shops of every description; had a donkey ride on "Yankee Doodle," as the day before we took a camel ride on a beast similarly named, of course for the time being for our American benefit.

The Nile, in appearance, is rather disappointing. It is muddy, and its banks, for the most part, are treeless. Of course this is the Lower Nile. The upper river I suppose to be quite different.

Everything at the Pyramids was exactly as I had fancied it. Ten miles south of the city, five miles back from the river on a plateau of sand-covered limestone ledges of rocks, — back from which sweeps the great Libyan Desert, a dreary waste, — stand these ancient tombs; for such only they are, despite all the elaborate theorizing of the books relating to them. They are not disappointing. Massive, majestic and impressive, they are speaking evermore of the aspirations of those old kings for immortality and perpetual remembrance.

By all odds, however, the most impressive and awe-inspiring objects I have seen in all my rounds are those six or eight mummies in the museum dating, beyond a question, from the time of Moses. The preservation is wonderful; teeth, hair, finger nails, knuckles, all intact, as if they had been animated within ten years. As we filed past their coffins, we could almost imagine ourselves at a regular modern funeral. At all events, my remembrance of the face of the coffined Lincoln, which I saw in Chicago, is that it was no more real to life than that of these old kings and queens. The long locks of one of the queens lie about her neck and shoulders, as if just taken down for a combing. Think of looking on the bared breast of old Pharaoh! That breast under which beat once the heart which it is said God "hardened." I thought surely the whole of the old rebel — not merely his heart — was here hardened enough!

Off for Jaffa.

And now we are really on board the ship, with Jaffa for our destination, and Jerusalem beyond tugging at our heartstrings. The blue, blue waters of the Mediterranean are beneath me; the long, low, flat, sandy coasts of Egypt, away at my right, are receding, and our prow heads for the city of Simon the tanner.

By to-morrow noon we should be in Rolla Floyd's landing-boats, and soon after I shall, I trust, be making my pilgrimage to the spot where lie the ashes of Amory Gale. What would not some Minneapolis people I know give to be with me there? I covet for them the melancholy privilege.

The sea on which we sail is just a little wavy, but the sun shines brightly, and the white crests smile their congratulations to my joyful, eager heart. "My feet shall stand within thy gates, O Jerusalem!" I doubt if any pilgrim ever coursed this sea with more eagerness and satisfaction.

What a Sabbath that next day will be if God will! What a sanctuary we shall have to worship in! Gethsemane, Mt. of Olives, Mt. Zion, Calvary, and the Hill of Ascension near Bethany.

February 27.

The shores of the Holy Land are before me. The outlines of Jaffa begin to appear, although a shower which is falling dims the view, and dampens the sentiment. Half an hour ago we caught glimpses of the hills of Ephraim, but now they have disappeared. Though the rain is unpleasant, the seas are calm, and our landing will be an easy thing.

The sun shines brightly on the whole coast line from Mount Carmel, on the north, to Ashdod, on the south. Jaffa's hilly mount, with red-tiled roofs,— really quite a city,— is about two miles distant. The native boats coming out from the shore begin to dot the sea. Beyond them a little white surf breaks on the rocks. Now the whole hill district of Samaria stands out distinctly, with a peak which some say is Gerizim, crowning all.

Landed! In a little German hotel in Jaffa. Sitting on the veranda of the hotel, just before me are acres and acres of orange groves, golden with their abundant harvest. They lie on the ground under the trees also, as thick as buttercups in a pasture. Yonder across the grove in the rear of the city, is a pond which in Solomon's time was a harbor, and where doubtless the cedars from Lebanon for the Temple were landed. Here Peter had his wondrous vision on just such flat housetops as are all around me. Here Tabitha was raised from the dead. Oh! it is a delight to feel that I am in *the Land*, and that on those blue hills of Ephraim and Galilee, now in full view in the distance northward, our blessed Lord often gazed.

The Ride to Jerusalem.

JERUSALEM, February 28.

I have had a long ride to-day, thirty miles from Ramleh through a cold, driving rain. I am at last in the Holy City; or I should say upon the edges of it, for in truth I have not yet even seen the walls. We arrived at about 4 o'clock this afternoon, and stopped at a hotel which is about a half-mile outside the walls, which are so hidden by numerous modern buildings, consulates, hospitals, schools, etc., that from appearances no one would dream we were near Jerusalem. Heavy mists and rain clouds are over the whole region; and so cold was I and tired, on arriving, that I decided to remain by the fire, and wait until morning before venturing out to see anything. I confess I was not anxious to have my first view of Jerusalem under such skies.

The spots we passed to-day on our mountain-climbing ride (for such it was, in a closed carriage) were Kirjath Jearim, the vale of Elah, Job's well, and Emmaus. Some of them are authentic. The vales through which we came were so full of interest and even beauty to me! The green barley and wheat fields, the numerous olive groves and vineyards on the terraced slopes, were to my fancy vocal with the voices of sacred personages of old. It being springtime, the country is surprisingly green, and really being rapidly recovered from its former waste and unproductive condition. The endless succession of billowy hills, rocky beyond conception, were very engaging to me. Once they were peopled with myriad towns and villages. The prophets saw and moved over and among them. They all spoke to me of thoughts unutterable. The carriage road is superb — like a Swiss road; and the ascent from Ramleh of 2,500 feet reminded me of a Swiss pass. Jerusalem itself is right up in the clouds, the climax of the thirty-mile gradual ascent. A singular sense of being at home possesses one in Palestine. I seem no more a stranger in a strange land. Our Lord long ago pre-empted all this, and what was and is *His*, and has long been so dearly familiar to my mind and heart, I now claim as mine in His name.

So real do the Scripture events now appear to me, that it verily seems as though, if I were to go early to-morrow morning to the sepulchre, I should meet Mary and the "Gardener" whom she met, clasped and adored. As we passed Emmaus to-day, but for the pouring rain, I should have climbed the hill to the old ruins of white limestone, almost expecting to have the Saviour reveal himself as risen, and making himself known in the breaking of bread. A strong, sweet satisfaction fills me to-night as I pray and lie down to rest. Who shall say He is not still here?

In the Holy City.

Sunday Evening, March 1.

My first day in Jerusalem! I woke early, with strange sensations of surroundings of more than dramatic interest. It was raining again; but after a hasty breakfast, I sallied forth to find W., who had taken quarters for us in the German "Johanniter Hospitz," within the city itself. I was glad to find, as I made my way into the street, that the city — the old, quaint, walled part — could not be seen at all.

I took a carriage, and rode to the Jaffa gate. Then dismounting, I entered through the walls, and found myself in a very narrow street of about fifteen feet in width, and for the most part not only walled in, but arched overhead, so that nothing can be seen of the city as a whole. Indeed, this is characteristic of all the streets of the inside city; you cannot see it for the houses, and especially for the overhead vaulted coverings, all of yellow limestone. The sun was beginning to shine. We resolved to make our way at once to the Mt. of Olives, in order to get the general view while the clouds were broken. So we entered the Via Dolorosa, which leads to the St. Stephen's gate, opening towards the mount, and started. The street leads downhill all the way, is paved with stone, with both a slope and, about every ten or twenty feet, a step down besides.

THE JOHANNITER HOSPITZ.

All along this way the stages are marked indicating the successive steps by which Jesus was brought to crucifixion, and inscriptions in Latin are engraved on the walls. For example, " In this place Pilate delivered Jesus that he might be crucified." "Here they plaited a crown of thorns." "Here the soldiers scourged him," etc. The "Ecce Homo Arch" is shown; the place where He fainted under His cross, etc. To be sure, much of this is traditional; but nevertheless you are morally sure that along this road at least the Divine Sufferer passed.

Emerging from the Eastern or St. Stephen's gate, the Mt. of Olives burst full upon us; much as I had fancied, only rather nearer the city than I expected. There at the extreme left was the Galilee knoll; there in the middle, the Hill of Ascension, so called, the former surmounted by a fine Greek church with a lofty modern tower of fresh yellow limestone, the latter occupied by a Mohammedan mosque and a minaret old and gray. Still farther to the right, was the Hill of Evil Counsel. Down deep in the valley between us and the mount, was the green valley of the Kidron, the little stream now flowing pretty full. Just beyond the brook lay the "Garden of Gethsemane," with its few disappointingly small olives and cypresses, enclosed by a higher and every way stiffer and more modern wall than I expected to see. There are two enclosures — one claimed by the Greek Church, and the other by the Roman Catholic, as the true Garden, each having its own wall. Of course here is clap-trap again, to extort money from travellers. Still, we know the garden to have filled probably the whole place, and it was affecting to behold it.

View from Olivet.

I had resolved not to cast a look back on the city itself until I should have reached the summit of the mount; and so I trudged on a good twenty minutes' climb up the mount, thinking of David's experience when he fled from Absalom up this same steep, and found my way to the minaret of the mosque, entered, and ascended to the top of the spiral stairway. I came out on the eastern side. Then there burst upon me first the rolling and rugged Wilderness of Judea, and beyond it the bright, glistening waters of the Dead Sea, which seemed not more than four miles away — really twenty. I could see perhaps twenty miles of its length, silvery and placid, with mists and rain clouds lifted far above it. Rising high and purple beyond it, was the wall of Moab, which mounted up, up, and stretched far away beyond in a range of real mountains.

Running my eye northward along the summit line, I could discern the semblance of a peak now and then, one of which might easily have been Nebo. From such a height Moses could readily have taken in, under clear skies, the entire limits of Palestine, from Beersheba to Hermon, and as far as to the Mediterranean.

The height and majesty of this range quite astonished me. The mists upon it were sufficiently dense, and enough smitten through with sunshine, to make it all entrancingly mysterious, and yet to reveal its full outlines.

Now letting the eye run downward from the heights north of the Dead Sea, the great Jordan plain lay in full view. Oh, what wealth of verdure filled it! Touched with the greater and lesser portions of fickle sunlight which played upon the fields, every tint of green was revealed, the deepest sea green, verging on emerald, prevailing.

> "Sweet fields beyond the swelling floods
> Stand dressed in living green."

I could see why Lot became enamored to pitch toward Sodom. The banks of the Jordan we could trace, and in places see its waters glistening. The view was fascinating. I could almost see John baptizing the multitudes; behold the " Lamb of God " emerging from the waves; and, through the long perspective of the ages, see Joshua leading his hosts down those majestic, far-away slopes across the dry water-course, and piling their memorial stones on the hither bank. 'Tis good to have seen the spots, even at such a distance and from a point of view not granted even to Moses.

I had almost forgotten to look at Jerusalem. Walking now around to the western side of the minaret, I took in at a glance the whole city. It was much as I had imagined, — gray, ancient, solemn and sublime with moral and spiritual suggestion; the walls a little lower than I had supposed; the Mosque of Omar disappointing; the Temple area smaller than I had fancied; and the surrounding mountains more impressive; the vales of Jehoshaphat and Hinnom just as I supposed; — the whole like a dream. I had to rub my eyes to test myself if it were really I that was viewing the most august city on earth, and from the very mount from whence our Lord ascended.

My time in the Holy Land was necessarily very brief, — a bare week, — only time to go from Jaffa to Jerusalem, to the Jordan, Dead Sea, Bethlehem, Solomon's Pools, and Bethany, embracing, of course, the environs of the Holy City, Gethsemane, the Mount of Olives, Calvary, the Church of the Holy Sepulchre, tombs of David, Absalom, Rachel, etc. But what a *holy week* it was to me! I seem to see it all still as ever present.

It is full spring, and the country is lovely with herbage and flowers. The plain of Sharon is like a great Minnesota wheat farm; the mountains of Judah, gray and rocky, are also richly sown with glowing scarlet anemones, shooting stars, and pink-fringed daisies; the vales on the way down to Jericho are as fresh as Vermont mountain slopes, except as these again are purpled with flowers more gorgeous than robes of Solomon; the plain of the Jordan is green and golden by turns, and mysterious with haze, with a lack of perspective also, that everywhere mystifies you as to distance; the Dead Sea is crystalline in clearness; the mountains of Moab lie over there majestic as a range of the Rockies, deeply seamed with gorges, capped with snow away northward towards Gilead; and even yet I can see the sun in all his glory just peeping over Nebo at me as he did at sunrise when he saluted me on Olivet.

We were beneath the gnarled old olives in sad yet lovely Gethsemane, — a garden yet, — and there had a little prayer meeting of our own; with uncovered heads communing with Him who there agonized for us. With singular success Canova has chiselled the scene of that awful night, in a fine bas-relief which is set in the chapel wall hard by. The moment he has chosen is that in which the cup has been drunk to its dregs, the exhausted Saviour just sinking with utter faintness, and the " angel appears strengthening him." Before the requisite aid is given, however, the angel seems to pause a moment to sympathize. The pathos is exquisite. It overmasters you. I have rarely seen a marble that so conquered me. Statues are usually so cold, so icy. This has warmth that is too deep for tears.

Bethany.

We took a Sabbath day's journey through Bethphage, over Olivet to Bethany. The people living there are a wretched sort; but the sight of the place, on the southward sunny slope of the mountains, is very pretty and winsome. As a suburb of Jerusalem, it is so retired and yet so conveniently near, I could readily see how Jesus might often seek its hospitable sympathy and restful retreat. The almond trees were in blossom close by the ruins of the traditional house of Simon. The bustling woman drawing water at the well, might have been Martha herself; and the woman with the soft, tender eyes, decidedly pretty, who stood at a door near by with a kindly "*Salaam*" and a bunch of keys in her hand, might have been Mary, had the scene not been suddenly spoiled by the words "backsheesh," which reminded me that the Arab is still in the land. The tomb in the rocks which they show you as that of Lazarus, might be authentic.

We drove to Solomon's Pools, twelve miles out on the road to Hebron, and returning we stopped at

Bethlehem.

Bethlehem is the loveliest place in Palestine I have yet seen. The place is much modernized. It has schools and missions, that lift it up much beyond the ordinary. The children are singularly clean and pretty, and everywhere greeted us with sweet smiles.

We peered into the well of David by the gate. We visited the Church of the Nativity, and especially the crypt beneath it where, beyond any reasonable question, our Lord had His lowly human birth. There is an awe about the place that I have not felt elsewhere. I did not much wonder that the woman we saw passing through the place knelt and kissed the very stones beneath the thirteen little lamps, which are always burning overhead.

Ascending to the flat roof above, we looked out over the historic plain where, ages ago, Ruth gleaned and Boaz loved, and David watched his flocks and thrummed his lyre; where other shepherds later tended flocks, as they do still; where angelic choirs visited our earth, and their chief spake to mortal simple men, and directed them to the spot where they should find their infant Lord. I do not wonder that angels chose that spot for the sublime and yet tender annunciation.

The fields, as we saw them, were green as emerald with the springing corn; patches of olive trees embossed it. "The Tower of the Flock" standing amid the fields marks the place as monumental. The hillsides all about, terraced to their summits for the myriad grape vines, lying golden to the sunlight, give the scene an imperial cast.

Just through the dip in the hills yonder on the eastern side, I got a peep of the Dead Sea glistening in the morning sun; and still beyond, the purple Moab hills loom loftily, like a dark background of the law beyond the gospel. Thank God, however, the gospel prevails!

It requires no stretch of fancy to hear again the angels sing over a spot like that, especially with nineteen centuries of the gospel triumph behind one, having witnessed its modern achievements clear round the earth, besides having all the notes in one's own soul.

Ramleh.

March 6.

We came on thus far last night, thirty miles towards Jaffa, preparatory to sailing to-day : so I finish from here, speaking only of the ride hither.

Going up to Jerusalem a week ago, we rode the entire distance in the rain. Still, the road was interesting, although under such conditions. Returning we came under the full glow of an afternoon sun ; and the beauty of even the barren hill tops, to say nothing of the green, green valleys, vocal with the murmur of mountain brooks, was exquisite.

Leaving the Holy City from the Jaffa gate, on the high northwest side, we were 2,500 feet above the sea. Passing out on the magnificent mountain carriage road, now completed, we first see a much loftier mountain away northward. — Neby Samuel, where the prophet was entombed. A little farther down, we come to Mephtoah — a village named in the Book of Joshua, marking the border line between Judah and Benjamin. An hour more, and we pass Emmaus, lying ruined on the right-hand slope. A little later, and we enter the reputed vale of Elah, and cross the brook from which David took the stones with which to slay Goliath. The vale lies between two lofty mountains, on the sides of which, possibly, the two armies were encamped. Later, we pass the ancient house of Obed Edom, and in a few minutes more Kirjath Jearim, from whence the ark was taken to Jerusalem.

Considerable Syrian villages, built of rich yellow well-hewn limestone, are on all these spots. Trains of camels entering or emerging from all these villages meet us on the road, loaded with olive oil, vegetables, charcoal and what not. Two hours more down, down, the steep, winding and picturesque descent, increasingly beautiful with flowers, as we approach the broad plain of Sharon, and we spy southward, through an opening in the hills, the ancient fortified stronghold of the Maccabees.

An hour more, and the town of John the Baptist's birth (?), now modernized, with French schools, etc., and ever beautiful, appears. Farther down, we get a peep into the valley of Ajalon ; and yonder, northward, between two mountain horns, we spy the pass of Beth-Horon, where Joshua took his stand in perhaps the most decisive battle in human history. Take that victory out, and there would have been no history of the Jews.

Now we are upon the great plain, — one vast wheat-field ; and yet northward again those bald elevations, that seem loth to part with us, mark the camping-place of Richard Cœur de Lion, on his crusade to gain the Holy Sepulchre. Oh! there is here a romance, nay, a divinity of charm, that holds you with a spell from the moment when, approaching from the sea, you sight the mount on which Jaffa lies, till you leave the land.

A grand climax it has made of my delightful round, and confirms the conviction, strong in me before, that the work of giving the gospel, which was here incarnated, to all the nations, is the very lowest aim that a redeemed mortal should set before him. There is something grander than a crusade to regain the sepulchre even of our Lord ; viz., a systematic effort to proclaim among all peoples the risen power of Him who emptied that sepulchre, both for himself and for those who in all lands believe on His name. THIS, THIS IS THE TRUE CRUSADE!

MISSIONARY BOOKS.

FOR EVERY HOME AND S. S. LIBRARY.

PAGODA SHADOWS; or, Studies from Life in China.

By ADELE M. FIELDE of Swatow, China. With introduction by Joseph Cook. 16 new illustrations. Cloth, 12mo., on fine paper. Price, postpaid, $1.00.

In her presentation of Chinese character, life and customs, Miss Fielde has struck out a new and successful path. From her intimate acquaintance with the Chinese, and especially by allowing the people so largely to speak for themselves, she has presented Chinese life in a vivid and impressive manner, which would not have otherwise been possible.

OUR GOLD MINE.

Sixth edition. By Mrs. ADA C. CHAPLIN. An illustrated story of our missions in India and Burma. Price, postpaid, $1.25.

Many are inquiring how they may gain some reliable information, in a condensed form, concerning the early history of our mission work, its progress and results up to the present time. This book tells who our missionaries were and are, when they were sent out, the fields occupied, the obstacles overcome, and the results reached. To any who have not had an opportunity to inform themselves, this book is just what they need.

MISSIONARY SKETCHES.

By Dr. S. F. SMITH, formerly editor of the MAGAZINE; author of "America," etc. Brought up to date by REV. E. F. MERRIAM. Sixth edition. Price, postpaid, $1.25.

It is invaluable to those who wish to prepare matter for the missionary concerts and the mission circles in our churches. There is no book that can fill the place of Dr. Smith's "Missionary Sketches." The name of the author is a sufficient guaranty for its historical accuracy.

FROM DARKNESS TO LIGHT.

By Rev. J. E. CLOUGH of Ongole, India. Illustrated. Price, postpaid, $1.25.

Though as intensely interesting and fascinating as a romance, this is a strictly true story, and contains descriptions of birth and wedding ceremonies, festivals to the gods, and many customs peculiar to the Telugus, never before published, thus fully supplying the want so often expressed for a more extended knowledge of this wonderful people.

MY CHILD-LIFE IN BURMA.

By Miss O. JENNIE BIXBY. Price, postpaid, 60 cents.

W. G. CORTHELL, Mission Rooms, Tremont Temple,
BOSTON, MASS.

THE HELPING HAND

is published monthly by the WOMAN'S BAPTIST FOREIGN MISSIONARY SOCIETY, and furnishes every month the latest facts of interest — their work, and that of the Society of the West, at home and abroad.

Single subscriptions per year, thirty-five cents, postage prepaid. In packages of four or more, *to the address of one person*, twenty-five cents each per year. THE HELPING HAND and THE KING'S MESSENGERS, to one address, forty cents.

Send all *subscriptions and money* to W. G. CORTHELL, Missionary Rooms, Tremont Temple, Boston, Mass.

THE KING'S MESSENGERS To Heathen Lands

is published monthly by the WOMAN'S BAPTIST FOREIGN MISSIONARY SOCIETY. It is illustrated and designed especially for young people and Sunday schools.

TERMS: One copy for one year, twenty-five cents. Two to twenty-five copies, *to the address of one person*, each, per year, fifteen cents; twenty-five or more, twelve and a half cents each.

Send *all subscriptions and money* to W. G. CORTHELL, Mission Rooms, Tremont Temple, Boston, Mass.

THE BAPTIST MISSIONARY MAGAZINE,

published exclusively in the interest of the American Baptist Missionary Union, is the oldest Baptist periodical in America. It contains the latest intelligence from the foreign mission-fields, together with editorials, and articles discussing questions relating to the enterprise of missions.

TERMS (postage prepaid): One dollar per annum. Ten copies and upwards, to one address, eighty cents per copy. The MAGAZINE and HELPING HAND, to one address, one dollar and fifteen cents; MAGAZINE, HELPING HAND, and KING'S MESSENGERS, to one address, one dollar and thirty cents.

THE KINGDOM

is published monthly by the Executive Committee, by order of the Board of Managers of the American Baptist Missionary Union.

Its aim is to give, in a condensed form, a summary of the missionary news of each month.

TERMS: Single copies, ten cents a year. Clubs of twenty and more, *to the address of one person*, five cents a copy per annum. Address "THE KINGDOM," Missionary Rooms, Tremont Temple, Boston, Mass.

THE BAPTIST MISSIONARY MAGAZINE.

The Only Organ of the American Baptist Missionary Union.

NOTICE CAREFULLY THE SIX DEPARTMENTS.

1. **EDITORIAL.**—In this department will be found items of special importance relating to the work of the Missionary Union, brief comments on current events in missions, and also articles on matters of general missionary interest.

2. **GENERAL ARTICLES.**—These will be chiefly original, contributed largely by our missionaries on the various fields, and by our ablest writers at home; but in order to give a wide survey of missionary principles and work, judicious selections will be made from other publications, on topics not fully covered by the contributions to the MAGAZINE.

3. **MISSIONARY CORRESPONDENCE** will contain letters from our missionaries on the various fields, giving such views of their work and experiences as will be interesting and important to those who stay at home to "hold the ropes."

4. **MISSIONARY OUTLOOK** consists of short selections upon important points relating to missionary work everywhere, and the progress of Christianity throughout the world.

5. **MISSIONARY NEWS** gives, under appropriate geographical heads, the most important and freshest items of missionary intelligence from all missionary lands, gathered from a careful reading of a wide range of missionary periodicals.

6. **DONATIONS.**—In this department the donations and legacies to the Missionary Union are acknowledged in detail for each month in the year.

TERMS.—Single Subscriptions, $1.00 per year. Ten copies or upwards, or clubs equal to 5 per cent of the church membership, 80 cents each. Clubs equal to 10 per cent of the church membership, 70 cents each. Copies sent to each individual address if desired.

THE JULY NUMBER of the MAGAZINE contains the Proceedings of the Annual Meetings and the Annual Report of the Union in full.

All who are interested in our foreign missions, and want to keep informed in regard to them, should take the MAGAZINE.

REV. J. N. MURDOCK, D. D., } *Editors.*
REV. E. F. MERRIAM,

Address BAPTIST MISSIONARY MAGAZINE,
TREMONT TEMPLE, BOSTON.

www.ingramcontent.com/pod-product-compliance
Lightning Source LLC
Chambersburg PA
CBHW020251170426
43202CB00008B/314